Counselling for Grief and Bereavement

Counselling in Practice

Series editor: Windy Dryden
Associate editor: E. Thomas Dowd

Counselling in Practice is a series of books developed especially for counsellors and students of counselling which provides practical, accessible guidelines for dealing with clients with specific, but very common, problems.

Counselling for Grief and Bereavement

Geraldine M. Humphrey
and David G. Zimpfer

SAGE Publications
London • Thousand Oaks • New Delhi

© Geraldine M. Humphrey and David G. Zimpfer 1996

First published 1996

 SAGE Publications Ltd
6 Bonhill Street
London EC2A 4PU

SAGE Publications Inc
2455 Teller Road
Thousand Oaks, California 91320

SAGE Publications India Pvt Ltd
32, M-Block Market
Greater Kailash – I
New Delhi 110 048

British Library Cataloguing in Publication data

A catalogue record for this book is available from the British
Library.

ISBN 0 8039 8403 0
ISBN 0 8039 8404 9 (pbk)

Library of Congress catalog record available

Typeset by Mayhew Typesetting, Rhayader, Powys
Printed in Great Britain by Biddles Ltd, Guildford, Surrey

Contents

Preface

This book starts from the premise that loss and grief are normal and integral aspects of life itself. Grieving is a process, not something to 'get over'. While a good share of the contents here relate particularly to death, we maintain that death is only one kind of loss to be grieved; there are also many other types of loss which one may be expected to cope with and to resolve. The materials here easily translate to a variety of losses that people experience.

Human service care providers rarely work with an individual who has not experienced some type of loss. A lifetime is an accumulation of losses; these may play upon each other as triggers or may ignite what otherwise might be considered an inappropriate or excessive grief response. In addition, losses are often ignored or not validated, and unresolved losses are often found to be at the root of later mental health problems. Any given loss is set in a context of a lifetime and cannot be seen as an isolated event.

Theory in human growth and development is offered as the foundation for the concepts of attachment, loss, and grief. Categories of loss, perspectives involved in the grief process, and a sketch of various bereavement models provide the content base for the reader. In the realm of service delivery, assessment and intervention strategies with plentiful case examples are given throughout the text. We attempt to offer concrete direction for providers to work with their clients in a manner that promotes healing and even a sense of growth. Special applications treated include instances of murder, suicide, AIDS, and early loss of a child. Since some losses can be foretold, attention is also devoted to anticipatory grief. In addition to individual counselling as a modality, other approaches are covered such as group work and outreach education programmes. Boundaries are spelled out in terms of ethical behaviour and in terms of acknowledging when a client's grief may be pathological or beyond the skill of the present practitioner.

The book is a practical guide for a wide range of help providers, including counsellors, social workers, psychologists, nurses, clergy, educators, and volunteers in social service agencies and schools. Education programmes for these providers typically do not acknowledge the complexity of the concept of loss, nor do they commonly provide adequate skills to facilitate the process of grief. Our contribution here is intended to be introductory to the field, and offers providers the opportunity to view loss and grief as an important specialized area of counselling.

Acknowledgements

I would like to acknowledge the Grief Support and Education Center, whose board, staff, students, and clients have enriched my life in so many ways over the last ten years.

I also want to thank Ben Hutton, Ed.D., who was there, in so many ways – as educator, supporter, colleague, father, and friend.

Lastly, I thank John. His unselfish love and support allowed me the opportunity to grow and experience life in a way that never would have been possible without him.

Geraldine Humphrey

My wife and I have lost two children to untimely and tragic deaths, one very young and the other in the prime of young manhood. Our own sense of loss and the accompanying mourning have been powerful personal experiences of what bereavement feels like, what it does to one's sense of being, and how it shakes one's values and challenges life's meaning. Though the opportunity these children have offered me is quite unwelcome, I must thank them. In addition, in my work as a counsellor with persons who have life-threatening illnesses, I deal with loss and grief on a daily basis. These clients are special in how they guide me on the path of helping them, and their service to me has been inestimable. Finally, I am indebted to my dear spouse, Lou, for her constant support and unfailing belief in me. Without her nothing I do would be easy; in fact, perhaps impossible. She is my rock.

David Zimpfer

1
Loss and Grief in Life

Loss is an integral part of life. It is not something that happens to us as we live; rather, it is life itself. Death is not the only loss a human might experience; yet it is often the only loss that is validated as a legitimate grief experience. In our view, any event that involves change is a loss that necessitates the process of grief and transition. A loss event requires that some part of the individual be left behind and grieved before the process of transition and rebuilding can occur.

Loss is defined as the state of being deprived of or being without something one has had, or a detriment or disadvantage from failure to keep, have, or get. Grief is the pain and suffering experienced after loss; mourning is a period of time during which signs of grief are shown; and bereavement, as discussed by Raphael (1983), is the reaction to the loss of a close relationship.

The bereavement experience includes the concept of grief, as pain and suffering must be experienced in order to heal and resolve the loss event. It also includes ideas of reaction, adaptation, and process. Reaction involves a response. The bereaved person reacts emotionally as the pain of grief is experienced, and gradually reacts cognitively and behaviourally as a new identity is formed and a life is rebuilt. Adaptation refers to the concept of letting go of that which has been lost, compromising, and gradually adjusting to and accepting a new life. And process involves the total experience. The work of bereavement is not linear; it is cyclical in nature, with many painful returns to the beginning to start the process once more. Tailspins back to an earlier stage of grief are an inherent aspect of the bereavement experience.

Effective resolution entails an active involvement. Loss, grief, and bereavement violate personal boundaries and remove a sense of security and control. The bereaved person will never have the same identity as before. He or she is no longer attached to a person, object, or activity that provided security, meaning, or purpose. Although this has the potential to be positive in terms of growth, initially a person feels a sense of aloneness and helplessness. Models of loss have evolved over time, including theories of attachment and ways to conceptualize the giving up of these attachments. Current models have moved from concern with mere coping towards interventions that foster growth and self-actualization. However, despite research and insight into this human condition, grief for many remains a passive process. Grief is often perceived as something to 'get over' in a fixed period of time. Yet we will come to understand in this book that process implies more than fixed tasks. Counsellors must continuously be aware that process involves trial and error, change, and frustrating returns to earlier experiences of grief. It demands an active response in order to restore one's sense of ability to be in control again. Moreover, loss cannot be narrowly viewed as one event. Each loss is influenced by past losses, and each loss will be affected by additional secondary losses that will occur as a result of the present loss at different times of the process.

In the discussion that follows, we will consider the evolution of models, as well as the categories of loss, and the perspectives that influence a bereavement experience. These ideas provide frameworks for assessment and interventions and will be referred to throughout the book.

Evolution of models of loss and bereavement

Models and theories have attempted to explain the complex process experienced after significant loss and change in our lives. Evaluating the models of bereavement over time shows more of an evolution of theory and practice than the creation of distinct models. The focus has moved from theories of attachment and loss, to concepts of acute grief, to tasks, to stages, to psychological processes and phases, and finally to Rando's model (1993) in which she incorporates numerous theories and integrates the various concepts into her Six 'R' Processes of Mourning that occur within three phases of grief and mourning. There are numerous models and it is beyond the scope of this book to identify all of them or to discuss any one in detail. The intent is to identify several that have been particularly influential and useful to persons who counsel others in their loss and grief.

From Freud on, there has been an emphasis on personal attachment to objects and people, and the giving up of some part of self following a loss (death or non-death) event. Attention to this loss of some aspect of self is an integral part of grief resolution; however, it is the part that is often negated and avoided today. During human history the experience of grief and its resolution has become more of a task to be accomplished, or something that must be got over and forgotten. The importance of healing the internal void within us, or that part of us that has been eliminated because of the loss, is not often understood as the foundation of self-restoration.

Freud offers one of the earliest models for consideration. He referred to the emotion present in melancholia as 'mourning', meaning that one is searching for an attachment that has been lost. Using the concepts of the ego and id, he discussed the need for the ego to disengage from that which has been lost and eventually to withdraw energy from the lost object. The bereaved was not grieving just one object; rather, he/she was grieving and letting go of multiple layers of attachments (stored memories and symbols) that are involved in the formation of a relationship. In a slow and arduous process, the reality of the loss is accepted by the ego and instinctual energy is withdrawn; thus the ego can accommodate the loss and search for new attachments. Although he does not provide a clear framework for operationalizing the process, Freud offers an understanding of the multiple levels of human attachment and the difficulty facing the bereaved who must undertake the task of grief work.

Lindemann's work (1944) is considered a milestone in the development of ideas about bereavement. His study was based on his interventions with 100 bereaved individuals, following the deaths of family and friends in the Coconut Grove night-club fire in the Boston area. In 1942, an accidental fire in the main part of the overly packed restaurant resulted in the deaths of over 500 people. After the disaster Lindemann provided opportunities for the bereaved survivors to work through their grief. From his interventions he gathered and studied data, which resulted in his study that offered a description of various symptoms of normal grief, with additional signs that he believed might indicate potential pathology. In the initial stages, he conceptualized acute grief as a normal part of the process. Lindemann proposed six characteristics of acute grief: somatic distress, preoccupation with thoughts/images of the deceased, guilt related to the deceased or the death event, hostile reactions, loss of function, and a tendency to assume traits of the deceased in one's behaviour. The last characteristic could indicate pathology in a later part of the process. In addition to these descriptions, Lindemann has provided a model and frame of reference that allows one to consider grief as work, with specific tasks to accomplish. His tasks included undoing emotional and psychological attachments with the deceased, readjusting to an environment without the deceased, and rebuilding new relationships.

Although Kubler-Ross was not the first nor the last theorist in this field, her name and stage theory are still the connection that many people make today when death and grief is the topic of consideration. Her landmark contribution, *On death and dying* (1969), came at a time in the history of the United States when stage approaches to psychological theorizing were acceptable and death was a taboo subject. She opened the doors to discussion and acknowledgement of death and to addressing the loss experience. Her focus was on those who were dying, not on those going through a bereavement process after a significant loss. Yet because of the simplicity of her stages, the ability to comprehend them, and the lack of visibility of other theorists in this field, hers is the theory and approach still most widely recognized today.

As a psychiatrist, she acknowledged her allegiance to the psychological concepts proposed by Freud. Noteworthy among these were theories of the unconscious mind, and the belief that the psychiatrist was more capable than the layperson of understanding and interpreting what was occurring in the unconscious mind. This recognition of her background is important, since the tenets of her stage theory are grounded in Freudian concepts. Stephenson (1985) critiqued Kubler-Ross's contributions to this field of study. He appreciated the fact that she opened pathways to communication of a subject that had been avoided; yet her psychoanalytical orientation has been a subject of debate. Her primary intention was to understand the experience of those who had a terminal prognosis and to facilitate a supportive process of coming to terms with one's mortality. As she and her assistants listened to over 200 hospitalized patients who were terminally ill, she interpreted what she heard and subsequently identified five predictable stages in those who are dying. Through these interviews, she interpreted their actions and emotions and delineated the stages of denial, anger, bargaining, depression, and acceptance. Today these emotions and behaviours are not viewed as separate entities in a linear progression; they are acknowledged as part of a larger and more cyclical process. Moreover, what is questioned today is the concept of the unconscious mind (i.e. whether or not it can control actions) and the ability of the psychiatrist to better understand the reality of the patient's experience (i.e. the patient is not in touch with an inner reality, because he or she has not been professionally trained).

Throughout her work, one finds Kubler-Ross interpreting

> the actions and emotions of the patient. All these interpretations in turn reinforce her theory. It is possible that over time the five stages ceased to be hypothesis and became a self-fulfilling prophecy. New information, if it came about solely through the subjective interpretation of Kubler-Ross, would only serve to reinforce her theoretical perspective. This is an all-too-common problem for the psychoanalytical school. (Stephenson, 1985: 89)

Debates in the counselling profession today focus on how accurate the counsellor can be in interpreting a client's experience, diagnosing, and prescribing treatment. Emphasis is turning towards the concept of co-facilitation of a process, with the client's perspective taking the lead.

Bowlby's Attachment Theory is another important landmark in this field of study. In three volumes entitled *Attachment and loss* (1969, 1973, 1980), he explores instinctive and attachment behaviours of humans and animals, the course of development (ontogeny) of human attachment, an ethnological approach to human fear, and the trauma of loss. In addition to his research, his clinical work with young children and adults (on issues of separation and grief) has provided a wealth of knowledge and a framework for interventions. His professional background was psychoanalytical; however, he broadened his theoretical groundwork to include cognitive psychology, developmental psychology, and ethnology. Cognitive psychology stresses that actions and emotions are a result of cognitions and belief systems. Developmental psychology is the framework for understanding an individual on the basis of his or her progression physically, mentally, and emotionally as compared to a chronological age and the developmental expectations for a particular age. Ethnology refers to the study of the characteristics and beliefs of communities and individuals.

Bowlby (1980) believes that attachments are developed early in life and have a basis of security and survival for the individual. When these attachments are endangered or broken, there is a normal human response of anxiety and protest. He bases much of his theory on findings from his work with children separated from their mothers. Papers written from the 1950s through to the 1980s reported findings from his infant studies that reflected the similarities between the responses of human infants and other high-order primates separated from their mothers. These similarities led him to believe that these responses had a biological basis, were instinctual and adaptational, and provided a basis for the survival of the species.

The conceptual framework that Bowlby (1980) brought to the study of mourning differed from what had been traditionally accepted. He believed that his new paradigm allowed him to dispense with some of the abstract concepts, such as psychic energy and drive, which he had found in the course of his research to be unsatisfactory. He stated that his attachment theory facilitated a way of understanding the distress and emotional disturbance experienced by humans when affectional bonds to particular others were broken. Underlying this theory is the belief that attachment behaviour is instinctive and mediated by a behavioural system that is developed early in life. This system is goal-directed and functions to maintain attachments. Attachment behaviour has the potential to remain active throughout life, and is often observed in situations of loss and grief that force bereaved individuals to fill painful voids and make new attachments. It should not be viewed as pathological in an individual after a significant loss; however, new attachments should not be sought with the intention of avoiding other aspects of the grief and mourning processes.

Bowlby also views mourning as including a variety of psychological processes that are set in motion by the loss of a loved one. He cites four general phases: numbing, yearning and searching, disorganization and despair, and reorganization. In addition to the phases, he discusses cognitive biases (cognitive structures) which filter information and serve as the mechanisms that form individual perceptions and belief systems. He hypothesized, based on his research findings of the role of attachment figures throughout life, that experiences with these early figures form cognitive biases and serve as the basis for patterns of relationship that a person makes throughout life. Moreover, he maintained that future losses would be influenced and processed by these cognitive biases.

Bowlby's interventions centre on cognitive insight and cognitive restructuring. He has emphasized the need to process information:

> For it is only when the detailed circumstances of the loss and the intimate particulars of the previous relationship, and of past relationships, are dwelt on in consciousness that the related emotions are not only aroused and experienced but become directed towards the persons and connected with the situations that originally aroused them. (1980: 200)

Once insight is gained and the cognitive and emotional aspects of relationships have been explored and experienced, the bereaved progresses towards changing cognitive constructs. How one viewed one's world and experienced it no longer applies. Life will never be exactly the same. Life can be meaningful again; however, this necessitates the creation of a new internal template of how one will view one's world.

Worden (1991) did not propose a new theory. His intention was to provide a practical application of established theory in counselling sessions. His book, *Grief counseling and grief therapy*, focuses on counselling for the tasks of grief and his contribution in the area of assessment and interventions has been recognized as a milestone in the field. His tasks of grief build on Lindemann's (1944) approach that delineated three tasks, and on Bowlby's conceptualization of attachment and loss. He views mourning as necessary and sees counselling as a facilitative process that allows the bereaved to identify four specific tasks of grief: to accept the reality of the loss, to work through the pain of grief, to adjust to an environment in which the deceased is missing, and to emotionally relocate the deceased and move on with life. Accepting the reality of the loss is a cognitive acceptance that the loss has occurred. Working through the pain of grief entails a willingness to fully experience the pain of grief and the additional pain that will emerge during the tasks of grief work. Adjusting to the environment in which the deceased is missing is a pervasive and continuous aspect of grief work. The environment is everywhere. It can be places, people, events, music, holidays, and so forth. The environment is ever-present and reminds one of one's loss. Lastly, to let go emotionally and to reinvest in life again does not mean forgetting, nor does it necessarily mean remarriage (for the widowed). It means that the bereaved realize that their emotional output to the deceased cannot be returned to them as it previously had been. When this realization is integrated, the bereaved cease continued attempts to get their emotional needs met from the deceased. They will begin to invest emotionally in other relationships or activities. For each of these tasks, Worden gives clues for identification (i.e. how far one has progressed in one's task work) and specific interventions to address each task. To him, grief counselling is the process that promotes a normal movement through these tasks; grief therapy, on the other hand, addresses areas of conflict and complication that might be hindering a normal process. Worden states that these issues of complication, if present, must be addressed first before the tasks of grief can be completed.

Rando (1993) has proposed her conception of the Six 'R' Processes of Mourning. She mainly addresses loss following a death, but states that her model may be generalized to other types of loss. Although there are some similarities to Worden's (1991) tasks, this model elaborates the grieving tasks and includes phases during which they might occur. Moreover, Rando broadens considerations for each task or process beyond what is implied in Worden's model, providing a more extensive base for assessment and intervention strategies.

AVOIDANCE PHASE: to **R**ECOGNIZE the loss. This includes both the cognitive acknowledgement that the loss has occurred and a meaningful understanding about the death or loss event.
CONFRONTATION PHASE: The bereaved must **R**EACT to the separation from that which has been lost. This includes fully experiencing the pain, finding appropriate expression for the full range of emotions, and identifying and grieving the secondary and symbolic losses that will emerge from the current loss event.
During this phase it is also necessary to **R**ECOLLECT and

reexperience the deceased and the relationship through reviewing and remembering. Lastly, during this phase, the bereaved must **R**ELINQUISH the old attachments to the deceased and the old assumptive world.

ACCOMMODATION PHASE: includes the processes of **R**EADJUSTING to a new world without forgetting the old, and **R**EINVESTING in meaningful life.

As specialists in this field, we (Humphrey & Zimpfer) have relied on concepts from the above models as well as others in the field. The above theorists have successfully built upon or elaborated upon past models, using creative innovations based upon their personal efforts in research and counselling. From our past and present experiences (Humphrey, as hospice programme coordinator, grief counsellor and educator, and Zimpfer, as cancer counsellor, researcher, and educator), we have observed that those who seek counselling support often have additional issues previously repressed. Our belief is that there is never just one loss event. There are the secondary and symbolic losses that follow; but even more significant are the past repressed losses that emerge to compound and complicate the present experience. Loss and grief must be approached from a sound basis of theory that involves an understanding of attachment and loss and the tasks of the stages of human development. But theory alone is not sufficient. Theory needs methods that provide for an in-depth understanding of the uniqueness of each bereaved individual. This book will not only explore concepts and heighten awareness of the impact of loss and grief in the lives of individuals; it will also instruct the professional in the use of various tools for assessment and intervention.

Categories of loss

There are several types of loss. Understanding these categories provides a framework that encourages the counsellor to examine and organize the effects of prior losses; to understand the full significance of the present loss(es), and to anticipate secondary or symbolic losses that could occur as a result of the present loss. Rando (1993) emphasizes the necessity to assess and address secondary and symbolic losses. She defines these losses as those which develop as a consequence of the first loss. This assessment is not meant to create an overwhelming situation for the bereaved individual who already feels out of control. The purpose is to help the counsellor more fully understand the present reactions and behaviours of the bereaved and to gain a more accurate understanding of what this loss means to them, given a more detailed understanding of their past loss experiences. Moreover, by anticipating potential secondary losses, we can educate, prepare, and plan more effective intervention strategies for coping and grief resolution.

The following discusses each of the categories of loss and offers examples that illustrate potential losses in each category.

Relationship loss

Relationship losses include (among many possibilities) the experience of death of a loved one, illness, divorce, separation, abandonment, rejection, abuse within what was expected to be a trusting relationship, moving geographically from parents or friends, and so forth. Any change in a relationship as we once knew it, perceived it to be, or experienced it, constitutes a relationship loss. Individuals experience loss in relationships in numerous ways:

> I am an adopted child. We moved sometimes twice a year, every year that I can remember. I never really had enough time to make a good friend. I have no close friend to confide in. (18-year-old male, after a suicide attempt)

> The divorce was bad enough; but then mom remarried and we moved into my stepfather's house. He has two kids that I hate. He never sees what they do; I'm always the one in trouble. Now mom is siding with him. I've lost her too. (15-year-old female)

Loss of some aspect of self

We cannot experience a relationship loss without losing an integral part of and sense of who we are. If there was a relationship, we have invested some part of ourselves in it. Who we view ourselves to be comes from the feedback in the interactions/dynamics of relationships. A major component of the grief process involves letting go of a former identity, grieving that part of you which is gone for ever, and rebuilding a new identity. This loss of some aspect of self not only occurs in relationships with others, but also in any situation that demands change in personal identity. In addition to the above, loss of some aspect of self is also experienced in child abuse, rape, illness, physical change, loss of hopes, dreams, and major change and disappointments. Professional burnout and professional impairment are profound losses of self. Losses of aspects of self appear in various ways:

> Biking was my life. When I wasn't biking, I was repairing cars or building something. I could never stand to see a person who was handicapped. Now I have to depend on others to wheel me

around in this chair. I was just starting my life; now it's over. (26-year-old paraplegic)

Everything I do is wrong. I can't keep a job, I can't get any control in my life. Everything I touch turns to dirt. (47-year-old male who had been laid off)

Treasured objects
Objects are physical and tangible; their significance is intangible. A treasured object is any object that connects one in reality or memory to an important relationship or some aspect of identity. Often they are objects that have been part of a family for generations, connecting that individual to part of his/her past and heritage. The family home that is sold after the death of parents often represents the loss of connection to childhood. Fire and theft often deprive individuals of treasured objects that have important significance. Loss of a lifestyle is an intangible loss in this category, and often occurs after a loss in another category such as divorce or death:

His death was one matter to get through. I don't even remember the funeral. The hardest thing was having to sell the camper. I can't afford to keep it. I don't even know how to drive it. Anyway, where would I take it? That was our camper and we travelled in it for the last 14 years. I feel like I'm losing more than a camper. (67-year-old widow)

I know we were lucky to get out alive; but 23 years of my life have just disappeared. I don't have a birth certificate, a driver's licence, or a social security card. Someone gave me a purse to use, but I have nothing to put in it. (50-year-old female, following a total loss of home and possessions after a fire)

Developmental losses
Developmental losses are a natural part of the life-cycle, and are often not recognizable. Growth, insight, and maturation are losses because change is involved and a part of self must be relinquished. Maturing, ageing, and physical changes can bring very poignant losses.

Developmental losses often compound or confuse more visible losses. A 65-year-old whose job position is eliminated is also coping with developmental issues of ageing and possible retirement. An adolescent being 'dumped' by a lover may also be experiencing losses inherent in that stage of development. A major loss during the adolescent period of development is to let go of carefree ways and to become responsible. And for children, who lose significant others

Life is loss, grief, growth . . .
A universal experience of
cycles and circles:

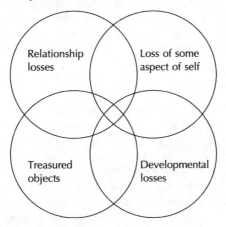

We must grieve to let go, to grow,
and to make future attachments.

Figure 1.1   *Categories of loss*

through death, the grief process may span their developmental stages. For children, at each new stage of development, the loss will be re-evaluated and new meaning will be integrated. Developmental losses can take many forms:

> For 20 years I was in charge of the entire department. In the new reorganization I am part of a committee. I don't even have a private office any more. I'm 58. I can't find a position elsewhere. I feel trapped and too old to do anything about my situation. (58-year-old female executive)

> I don't know if I can handle growing up. I'm so stressed right now. I think it's only going to get worse because after I graduate I'll have to get a job and be responsible for taking care of myself. If I can't handle the stress of college, how will I ever handle being an adult? (20-year-old female)

The categories of loss overlap. Figure 1.1 serves as a visual aid that allows the counsellor to educate the client about losses in life that might not have been considered as contributors to the present grief experience. This matrix would first be used as an assessment device by the counsellor, as he/she listens for additional past, present, and potential future losses that will influence and impact the presenting issues of loss. Several sessions into the counselling process, it can then be used as an educational tool in assisting the client to reflect upon his or her life and gain insight into the pervasive nature of loss. Case examples throughout the book will offer additional possibilities.

Perspectives on loss

The counsellor needs a framework to more fully understand the experiences of loss and grief. The framework becomes a holistic tool that allows one to gain fuller access to the client's private world of grief and his/her unique experience of it. It must be remembered that no two people will experience the same loss event in the same manner. Our framework comprises several perspectives, including the philosophical, spiritual, psychological, sociological, and physical.

It is important to be aware of these various perspectives and how they influence a client's frame of reference and grief experience. Not all the perspectives may emerge or be relevant at any one time. Some, however, may emerge several times during the process and be more influential. The influence exerted and the contributions made by each perspective can be positive or negative.

Philosophical perspective

Philosophical issues are always a part of a grief experience. How an individual lived and previously interacted with his or her world no longer makes sense. Numerous questions about the meaning of one's existence emerges. Attention to the category of loss of some aspect of self is important here. How much of the invested self that has been lost because of this event is a pivotal issue in rebuilding? Is this individual willing and capable to look within and find new dimensions of self? This question becomes the foundation of ongoing assessment and subsequent intervention strategies. Moreover, loss of some aspect of self also draws attention to the fact that death becomes personalized and real for the survivors. One can no longer hide behind the cloak of immortality.

This perspective introduces difficulties of aloneness, meaningless-ness, despair, responsibility, and existential anxieties. From a philo-sophical perspective, one can consider each loss event in life as part of the eventual process of coming to terms with our own mortality. Avoidance of grief after any loss or change event can be viewed as part of the difficulty humans face in reflecting upon core issues of their existence and eventual demise. Every loss involves change and letting go that needs to be processed. Theorist Ernest Becker (1973) asserts that man can live more fully and authentically when he faces this ultimate reality. He postulates that the anxiety experienced after any loss has the fear of one's own death at its core.

Spiritual perspective

Clients are influenced by their spiritual beliefs (or lack of them). As the categories of loss are explored and a number of losses identified, it is often observed that the spiritual realm is the only emotional anchor left for survival. Belief in an afterlife can provide reason for going on and hope for reunion with a loved one. However, spiritual beliefs and/or the tenets of organized religions may also be the source of fear and guilt. Often individuals may believe that a loss is a sign of punishment from God for some wrong that has been committed. With this belief, additional guilt is often imposed upon the grief, and the bereaved can have a tendency to see themselves as bad and not worthy of forgiveness for past wrongs. An understanding of this perspective in a client's life is essential. During times of loss, conflicted beliefs or a lack of spirituality can become additional issues for an individual.

A lack of spirituality exerts a different kind of influence. Although guilt may not be experienced, there is often a deeper sense of meaninglessness and lack of perceived purpose in life. Those without a belief in someone or something beyond the human dimension often verbalize regrets that they have nothing to 'hang on to' or to 'fall back on' during this time of loss. Many have said that they envy the strength and comfort that faith and hope provide for those who have a sense of spiritual connectedness and beliefs.

Although the philosophical and spiritual perspectives overlap, there are some differences. When considering the latter, there is more of a focus on an individual's relationship (or lack of) with God, a higher being, or some cosmic consciousness. Affiliation with an organized religion should not be the only consideration here. Many consider themselves religious or spiritual, but do not participate in formal, community worship. Jackson states:

> Religion has many facets, but in the complex creations that are a part of the religious consciousness, there has always been a clear pattern of seeking to speak to the deep anxiety within man that seems to be incident to his mortality. . . . Anxiety usually emerges when there is a threat to man's value system. Religion seeks to provide a value system that counters that threat by making man aware of a dimension of his being that is not merely biological or chemical or mechanical, but by its very nature has about it already the element that transcends mortality by being in tune with the infinite and eternal. It does this in part by expanding

man's perspective so that while he is in life, he sees beyond it. Religion seeks to give to man's life a cosmic status, so that, in the presence of things that might make him feel helpless and hopeless at one level, he can rise above those events so incident to his biological death and the existential threat to his being. (1977: 78–79)

Whereas the philosophical perspectives bring these existential questions and anxieties to the surface for an individual, the spiritual attempts to provide answers, direction, solace, and a potential opportunity for immortality (i.e. to live on in an afterlife).

Psychological perspective

The loss of some aspect of self is a core issue to be explored. If one has invested a part of one's identity and energy, this is a loss that has to be acknowledged and grieved. Included in this perspective is the loss or compromise of meaningful roles. Contributing factors include personality, coping styles, affective and cognitive domains, present stressors, and overall mental health.

Another consideration within this perspective is the idea that relationships are not created in a linear fashion. Raphael (1983) discusses the psychological work of undoing the bonds that created the relationship. She discusses this task as a process of reversing all that has gone into building a relationship. The many layers that were internalized into the complex, multidimensional image of the loved one or role are now reviewed. Moreover, the emotional components that made it valuable (positive) or painful (negative) must also be reviewed. Until one can address the multiple levels of connectedness, it is difficult to address the normal tasks and processes of grief.

A poignant example of this is the grief of a parent following the death of a child. The layers of a parental relationship are often complex and conflicted. There are few other relationships that demand such an investment of self and have as much potential for complications following the end of a relationship. It should be noted at this point that death is not the only loss that can sever the parental relationship. Parent–child disagreements can end in broken relationships, necessitating a grief process. One mother whose adult son had been estranged from her for over ten years could only remember the young, innocent boy who played so well with others. She dwelled on these memories, would not discuss the problems of his adolescence, and lived for the day that he would surely return to her. She was experiencing a tremendous loss and needed to carefully review, grieve, and reconstruct each aspect and year of their relationship. There were layers of experiences and memories that had been denied and avoided. Some layers had been too painful at the time (and continued to be); thus, more pleasant memories from the past were selected and focused upon. However, grief demands that the painful, avoided reality be reviewed, grieved, and released. Without partaking in this part of the process, she was not able to cognitively and emotionally integrate all aspects of the relationship in order to facilitate an incorporation of her son in healthy memory, and foster resolution of her grief.

Sociological perspective

This perspective greatly influences how one grieves or fails to grieve, and encompasses the impact that one's culture has on the bereaved. A culture/society establishes norms, many of which are unspoken but exert subtle (or not too subtle) pressures for conformity and prescriptions for belief systems and behaviours. Today we are influenced by past and present cultures; and as we look towards a new century, there is evidence of ideological shifts and some return to former beliefs and behaviours. There is a growing opinion that the emphasis on scientific rationality for answers in this century has created new problems that need new solutions. Within the field of loss and grief work, there is a growing awareness of the need for support systems, renewed emphasis on spirituality (a view especially held from a fundamentalist religious standpoint), and a return to the use of rituals during times of loss and transition.

In the sociological perspective it is also important to consider the nuclear family, the family of origin, support systems (real and perceived), ethnicity, socio-economic status, gender, religion, and other variables central to one's culture and frame of reference. Individuals will always refer to these factors in order to make sense of the loss experience. It is often the lack of support systems and the loss of religious and ethnic rituals that pose current problems for grief resolution. In the past, a shared cultural background often provided the environment that not only prescribed rituals of mourning, but also fostered the process of grief within an emotionally close community of family and friends. Changing societies have altered the make-up of these communities. Individuals can cognitively refer to their roots, but from a behavioural vantage point there is little opportunity to enact traditional rituals without the availability of the extended family or background culture.

Lastly, societies are becoming multicultural. This is a factor that may require additional education for the counsellor in order to understand the world of the client and be effective in the process. Multicultural issues are an inherent part of many clients' experiences of loss and grief, and are often negated or disenfranchised by the counsellor who is not perceptive. Counsellor training, in the past, has reflected the norms of the dominant society; diagnoses have often been influenced by social and cultural prescriptions of that society.

Physical perspective

This perspective includes all aspects of biology, physiology, pharmacology, and general functioning of a bereaved individual.

From a medical perspective, Engel (1961) proposes that loss and its resolution are integral aspects of homeostatic balance. He views the grief process as parallel to the process necessary for healing after a physical illness. Engel does not pathologize grief. He views it as a normal function that requires time and attention, with a distinct focus on difficult emotional tasks.

Grief can also mask itself in somatic complaints. It is essential to rule out physical problems, but the bereaved will not succeed if they try to find answers and solutions solely through physical diagnosis and medication.

The case study that follows is that of a client who initially came to counselling to cope with depression that resulted after she had broken her arm. It illustrates the potential that one event has to open up past losses and to activate additional losses. The case study is an example of the application of the various perspectives and the positive and negative influences that they can have on the loss experience.

The suicide of Jane: a lifetime of losses

Jane presented herself in counselling following a brief hospitalization for depression. She was 33 years old, married with two male children aged seven and nine. They were members of a close-knit, supportive Mennonite community. Jane was the church organist/pianist and was involved in restoring their century-old farmhouse. She was talented and intelligent. Her husband was self-employed, passive, and withdrawn. A broken arm necessitated that she have surgery and intensive physical therapy. About six months later it was discovered that the surgery had been unsuccessful and her bones had fused in such a way that she would never again have the full use of her right hand and arm. Moreover, her fingers would not be able to stretch sufficiently to play the piano. Depression set in and, following a brief hospitalization, counselling was initiated. The physical loss triggered many issues within the psychological perspective. Loss of roles and identity were aspects that emerged continuously, each time prompting new awareness of past losses and unresolved grief. Deprivation of an early attachment figure proved to be the base of the emerging pathology. Counselling spanned five years, with several hospitalizations and an extended stay in a mental institution. There were multiple suicide threats over the years and attempts at divorce and separation from her husband. There was intense involvement in her life by friends, family, church, and mental health professionals. From a sociological perspective there was an available community of support. However, to Jane these support systems no longer had meaning or influence. Finally, during a period when it appeared that her life had settled down, she went out one morning and completed her suicide in the manner that she had always threatened.

Many issues surfaced during the five years in counselling. The unsuccessful surgery on her arm opened hidden doors deep within her, revealing a broken human being who had never healed from losses. She had gone through the motions of living, appearing normal to all around her. She was a pleasant, gentle, and caring woman who was involved in church, community, and family. Her damaged arm became her noose. First she realized that she would never again be able to play the piano. Her music was a major part of her identity and a vehicle for expression of feelings that had never been consciously identified or verbalized. Because of her disabled arm, she could not continue with the renovation of her home, which was another creative outlet for her. In her depression, she began to distance herself from her children. She withdrew her nurturing and turned the responsibility of her two boys over to her husband. She then became overwhelmed with guilt. This action also raised the repressed reality that her mother had never wanted her or nurtured her. In the counselling process she shared poetry and creative writings from high school. She fully realized that she was an intelligent woman who had never had the opportunity to go to college because of finances and her predominant ethnic and religious culture that dictated many of her choices after high school. She explored with her counsellor the possibilities of attending college. She was accepted, and qualified for full financial aid. The day before signing up for classes, she attempted suicide. This process repeated itself many times over the next several years until her successful completion. Solutions for her issues were mutually arrived at in counselling sessions; however, she always sabotaged potential plans. Behaviours such as this were influenced by cognitive distortions, stemming from childhood. It became evident that this was an individual whose spirit had been broken early in life. She was not going to grieve, let go, resolve her pain, and rebuild her life. She was not wounded; she was broken, and would never heal. Her solution was suicide. The professionals were only capable of prolonging the living process. From a philosophical perspective, she never moved past an overwhelming sense of aloneness, meaninglessness, and despair. Spiritually, she had rejected her church, and on a deeper level she found no relevance or hope in a personal relationship with a God or a higher being.

Losses in retrospect were obvious. Grief issues were addressed in counselling as they emerged. Losses had been built upon losses. All categories of loss were revealed. Relationship losses had not occurred through death, but resulted from the absence of early nurturing and meaningful relationships. Loss of aspects of self were more apparent. The physical injury resulting in the loss of the ability to play the piano was the catalyst that brought past losses of identity into awareness. Loss of treasured objects emerged as secondary losses. Jane was unable to keep her job, which required physical labour. Hospitalizations after suicide attempts depleted the family's financial resources and the church's. All of this led to bankruptcy and the subsequent loss of their home.

Applying human development theory, it was judged that normal childhood developmental stages were never successfully achieved. Erikson (1968) outlines stages of development that need to be accomplished for healthy adult functioning. Resolution of early stages such as trust versus mistrust, autonomy versus shame or doubt, initiative versus guilt, or industry versus inferiority were never completed. Ongoing assessments revealed multiple unresolved developmental issues in Jane's life. Losses in this category centred around the lack of completion of these stages and the subsequent loss of psychological health.

We can learn from Jane how complex and interwoven the loss experience can be. We gain a clearer understanding of the potential and power of accumulated losses throughout an individual's life. We study this case to understand the depth and loneliness of one individual attempting to cope with a multitude of losses. Awareness of issues of loss will increase counsellor sensitivity and enable more in-depth and accurate assessment and intervention strategies. Education regarding loss and interventions for future mental health must be addressed from childhood onwards.

2

Assessment Strategies

The purpose of assessment is to gain entry into the client's inner world and to understand the unique experience of grief as influenced by present and past losses and the contributions from the various perspectives. Assessment is an ongoing process and should never be considered to be completed simply because the initial diagnosis has been done. Assessment and intervention go together throughout the sessions, with one paving the way for the other. Assessments allow for the next interventions to be planned; and interventions facilitate change, which prompts new issues to emerge.

Various tools can be utilized to gather information about each client and the significant issues surrounding each loss event. These range from intake forms, to a specific line of questioning around the perspectives, to describing a history of loss, to the use of tools from other models (e.g. Worden's tasks), to tests that measure depression, anxiety, quality of life, and so forth. Not every tool needs to be used with every client. Different tools are available to gain access and understanding when, in the professional judgement of the counsellor, something needs clarification or further understanding. The most important assessment and intervention tool will always be the counsellor. Without good clinical judgement and skills, external tools can be a hazard; they are often interpreted literally and at face value, misjudging the reality of an individual and his or her reactions to a loss.

Pre-counselling assessment

The first assessment starts with the telephone call from the client requesting counselling services. A pre-counselling intake form (Table 2.1) is used. This form identifies the type of loss; whether or not the client is currently receiving other counselling services; what the current feelings are; and if there are personal changes in habits such as eating, sleeping, or alcohol/drug use. After a significant loss many express feelings of not wanting to live any more. An initial assessment is necessary to determine if the statement is within the normal grief experience or if there is a level of lethality to the suicidal ideation. Other questions help to determine the mental and emotional

Table 2.1   *Pre-counselling intake form: to be completed during initial phone call, requesting counselling*

NAME _____

PHONE NUMBER: (HOME) _____ (WORK) _____

WHAT IS THE CONCERN YOU WANT ADDRESSED THROUGH COUNSELLING? _____
(For example, death, divorce, loss of job, etc.)

_____

_____

WHEN ARE YOU AVAILABLE FOR APPOINTMENTS? _____

REFERRED BY: _____

ARE YOU PRESENTLY RECEIVING COUNSELLING SERVICES? _____

ARE YOU PRESENTLY FEELING ANY OF THE FOLLOWING:

     DEPRESSED   ANGRY   LONELY   SUICIDAL

INTAKER'S INFORMATION

CALL RECEIVED BY: _____

DATE: _____ TIME: _____

DID CALLER SEEM TO NEED COUNSELLING AS SOON AS POSSIBLE? _____

ANY DETAILS THAT YOU THINK PERTINENT:

CLIENT ASSIGNED TO:

DATE: _____ TIME: _____

COUNSELLOR'S SIGNATURE: _____

status of the client and the need for immediate intervention. A question on gender preference may be added, as a number of clients have suffered some type of abuse but hesitate to request a male or female. Having some of this basic information before seeing the client for the first time allows the counsellor time to reflect on potential issues and what direction to pursue during the formal intake. If the client is in a state of emotional crisis, the counsellor may decide not to do a formal intake, but to address the present needs of the client immediately.

The counselling intake form (Table 2.2) is completed by the client on the first visit, but before the intake session. At times the counsellor will have to assist the client or clarify the information being requested. Intake forms for other types of loss are similar. The last part of the form can be changed to address specific issues of each loss.

Table 2.2 *Counselling intake form*

BACKGROUND: DATE _____

NAME _____ BIRTHDATE _____

ADDRESS _____

PHONE: Residence _____ Work _____

AGE _____ SEX _____ OCCUPATION _____

WHO REFERRED YOU TO THIS OFFICE? _____

IN YOUR OWN WORDS, WHAT IS THE MOST DIFFICULT THING FOR YOU NOW? _____

_____

WHO LIVES AT HOME WITH YOU NOW? _____

IF YOU HAVE FAMILY (NO LONGER LIVING AT HOME) PLEASE COMPLETE THE FOLLOWING:

Family Member's Name	Age	Sex	City of Residence
1.			
2.			
3.			

ARE THERE ANY OTHER PERSONS WHO ARE EMOTIONALLY SUPPORTIVE AND AVAILABLE TO YOU?

Name	Relationship
1.	
2.	
3.	

ARE YOU CURRENTLY RECEIVING MEDICAL CARE? _____

IF YES, BY WHOM? _____

ARE YOU CURRENTLY TAKING ANY MEDICATIONS? _____

ARE YOU CURRENTLY RECEIVING ANY ADDITIONAL COUNSELLING? _____

NUMBER OF YEARS THAT THERE WAS A RELATIONSHIP WITH THIS PERSON OR ACTIVITY _____

SIGNIFICANT DATES THAT HAVE THE POTENTIAL TO TRIGGER GRIEF REACTIONS (Examples: holidays, birthdays, anniversaries, special events)

DATE THAT RELATIONSHIP ENDED _____

Perspectives on loss

Designing questions around various perspectives on loss (Table 2.3) initiates the counsellor's process of joining with the client in order to more fully understand the totality of the individual's grief experience. Table 2.3 illustrates the several perspectives discussed in Chapter 1, with different loss examples given for each perspective. In an actual assessment, the counsellor takes the one loss issue presented initially by the client, and pursues the line of questioning across each perspective.

Table 2.3 *Perspectives*

Considerations of perspectives	Philosophical	Spiritual	Psychological	Sociological	Physical
	Loss of a 40-year friendship	Rape of a daughter	Heart attack – 43-year-old male	Executive's position restructured	Hysterectomy and other future, physical losses
Early counselling sessions (acute)					
A. Contributions to present loss	'I feel totally alone. I don't trust, and I have cut myself off from everyone.'	'How could God allow this to happen?' Questions existence of a God.	'Exercise was my way of feeling in control. I can't even do that now. My heart has failed me. I did everything right. This is not fair.'	'Every morning I come in and have to walk down the hall, past my old office, back to a room that five of us now share.'	Dealing with hysterectomy and symbolic losses from that, plus lack of recognition and support, triggers additional physical (medical) problems.
B. Contributions from past losses	Loss of two adult siblings – felt loss of connections to childhood.	No past losses – strong religious upbringing.	Past problems with business, but always regained a sense of control.	Change in past had always been a choice. Sacrifice of a personal life had been made for this sought-after position of power.	Death of brother – physical symptoms of severe headaches.
C. Interventions	Listen and validate. Continue to assess for other contributing factors to this perspective.	Don't challenge anger towards God. Give permission for feeling. Continue to assess spirituality.	Validate concerns. Assess for other coping mechanisms and irrational beliefs.	Assess for other sociological aspects and current support systems. What are the inbred cultural messages?	Education re: disease process and the 'mind–body' connection. Validate disenfranchised grief.

Middle counselling
sessions (chronic)

A. Contributions to
present loss

B. Contributions
from past losses

C. Interventions

Later counselling
sessions (reinvesting
and rebuilding)

A. Contributions to
present loss

B. Contributions
from past losses

C. Interventions

Initial assessment: illustrates various examples of loss. Examples correspond to Chapter 2 on assessment. Shows an application of the perspectives.

Continue to use this format as shown on page 22

Philosophical

Questions should explore how this loss has affected the client's outlook on life; if there is a personal philosophy that is helping at this time; what holds meaning and purpose at this time; if there is any sense of connection or relation to anyone or anything; if there have ever been similar feelings from past losses; what questions about life this loss has triggered; and what this loss has made the client more aware of. These questions are not all-inclusive; rather, they suggest a starting point. Additional assessment questions concerning this perspective will be generated by clients' responses to the counsellor's initial queries.

Illustrating the philosophical perspective, the following is an excerpt from an initial assessment with a 71-year-old female, Jean, whose presenting issues were the losses within the last two years of two adult siblings and a daughter-in-law (death), and the loss within the last year of a 40-year friendship that she and her husband had shared with another couple (non-death). She chose to focus on the relationship loss, because to her it was the most personally devastating and the one that she could not comprehend. Jean explained the nature of their relationship with this couple, which in retrospect had been too exclusive and demanding. They had allowed this couple to plan most of their social lives. Over the years, Jean realized that they had gradually shut out other friends, and now she did not feel that she had the right to regenerate those friendships which she had allowed to slip away. Moreover, she had lost trust, felt betrayed, and was not willing to take many risks with other people. With this other couple they had lived in the same town, and raised children together; and since retirement, they had spent the winter months in Florida in the same condominium. About two years prior to the ending of the friendship, her friend's husband started making advances towards her. After she told him to stay away, untrue stories began to be circulated about them by their 'best friends'. At the same time Jean's friend had been undergoing chemotherapy for cancer, and she did not want to create an extra burden on her by confronting her with the fabricated rumours. Their friends drew away, and Jean and her husband had little choice but to back away also. As she reviewed the sorrow and pain of the past year, she realized that because she no longer trusted anyone, she had withdrawn from life in general. Her world had become very narrowed, and she seldom did anything outside the house. Depression had set in, and a once lively and social woman had become a recluse.

> *J*: I feel totally alone. My husband says to forget them, but it is not that easy. Forty years of total investment can't be forgotten that easily. And I really can't talk to my husband about

how I feel; he has had several heart attacks, and I'm afraid to cause him stress from my feelings.

C: Forty years of caring, spending exclusive time with someone means that much of your energy and identity went into this relationship. You must feel like a lot of you is missing. Part of your grief is the personal loss of all that you gave of yourself in this friendship.

J: I told her everything and shared things with her that I never could share with my husband. There's no one in my life that I can do that with now. I feel totally alone. I don't trust anyone, so I've cut myself off from everyone. I can't seem to find any meaning or purpose from day to day, so I do nothing but cry.

C: You feel very alone in your grief.

J: Yes, I've had a lot of loss in my life, but I have never felt this devastated. I could always bounce back; but nothing makes sense any more. Why would something like this happen to us in our old age? We always cared about people and were good to them.

Jean initially focused on the lack of meaning and purpose, and the unfairness of what had happened to them. She had viewed the world realistically in terms of loss in life; however, the unfairness and injustice of this loss posed an existential dilemma regarding the nature of what had been done to them during a period when she and her husband should have been able to enjoy retirement and the company of lifelong friends.

Spiritual

This perspective encourages questions around the client's relationship with God or a higher being. This does not necessarily mean that a client will be a member of an organized religion. Questions posed range from directly asking a client if he or she believes in God and an afterlife and if this loss has affected or changed their relationship with God, to indirect questions about their conception of sin and punishment, or about possible affiliations within a church community. For example: 'What type of support are you presently getting from your church, what would you like to get from your church, what rituals (through your church) have you used that have been meaningful and helpful, what religious beliefs sustain you the most during these times, have your religion or spiritual convictions helped you through past losses, and are you presently experiencing any personal conflicts between your thoughts and emotions and your spiritual beliefs?' Again, it is necessary to state that these questions provide a beginning for the assessment of this perspective. They are not all-inclusive.

The rape of one's child is a loss that often directs the focus towards the spiritual perspective. Henry came for counselling after the rape of his 15-year-old daughter in a church camp by one of the male camp counsellors. He was doubly enraged: angry at God for allowing this to happen and furious that it happened within a church setting that presumably taught values of right and wrong. This was his third and youngest daughter; the older two had also attended this camp during their high school years. He confronted the administrative personnel at the camp, and they refused to believe that one of their staff members had been involved in this alleged rape. They insinuated that Henry's daughter had fabricated the story. Henry tried to go higher up in the hierarchy of the Church to get help, but continued to get the same response of denial on their part. Feeling alone, defeated, and violated, he left the Church of which he had been a lifelong member. He secured a lawyer to investigate his case.

　H: How could God allow this to happen, and within a church of all places? I have so much fury burning inside of me that I don't know what to do with it.
　C: Sometimes it helps just to share it with another person. I can't change what has happened, but I am willing to listen and to help you find ways of getting your anger out.
　H: We are good people. Why would God allow this to happen? I always believed that if you obeyed His commandments and lived good lives, He would watch over you and care for you.
　C: It is really hard when your religious upbringing has taught you certain truths and now you have to live with a different reality.
　H: Now I even question if there is a God; and if there is, will He punish the man who raped my daughter?

Anger directed at God, the question of whether or not a God exists, and the belief that God should protect the good are common grief responses, especially after a rape, when one feels so violated. It is important to listen and resist giving personal statements of your religious beliefs. Responses to the client at this time should be non-judgmental and reflective of what the client has expressed to you.

Psychological
This is a pivotal perspective that continues to emerge throughout the entire grief experience. Different aspects of this perspective will demand attention at varying times, often causing the client to feel drained of energy, unable to think or function. It will be important, early in the assessment, to listen for styles and characteristics of personalities, and to assess both pre-morbid and present personalities

of the clients. Ask the clients if they view themselves as having a different personality before the loss event. Use questions that encourage responses that provide information about clients in relationships with others and about their own sense of personal worth. Listen for responses that might indicate personalities that are dependent, histrionic, narcissistic, compulsive, and the like. A client's personality and how he/she views himself or herself is an important criterion in resolution of loss and grief.

Assessment of the affective and cognitive domains is an ongoing part of the counselling sessions. Early in the assessment determine the primary and/or current grief emotions and how the client expresses these feelings. Many admit to suppressing, avoiding, denying, negating, and rationalizing most of their feelings when they begin to emerge. Some fear total loss of emotional control if they were to allow expression of these feelings. Others operate on faulty cognitions, such as grief is a sign of weakness, emotion means self-pity, or that you should keep your feelings to yourself. Inappropriate affect (e.g. smiling as one relates a tragedy) is another clue that needs further exploration. Perhaps the client believes that it is important to maintain a certain outward countenance, or perhaps the client is not in touch with his or her emotions.

The belief that one should not or cannot express emotion affects the emotional status of a client as well as his or her mental abilities. Many with suppressed emotions develop more negative thoughts, lack ability to make decisions, and cannot find ways to cope with additional stress. Ongoing cognitive assessment is a key variable throughout the counselling sessions. Early assessment needs to determine the present status of cognitions and the ability to make decisions; moreover, a goal of assessment is to identify lifelong belief systems and possible cognitive distortions. What is the client's pattern of self-talk? What distorted or negative messages about himself or herself are continuously being reinforced? Within this cognitive assessment, it is often necessary to do a mental status exam that might identify impaired functioning, disorientation, or drug or alcohol involvement.

Psychologically, it is also important to assess the nature of the relationship that has been lost, what functions had been provided by this relationship, and what roles have been changed. Develop questions that bring out the stored symbols and inner images of the layers and meaning of this relationship. Symbols stored (or inner representations of how that relationship was perceived and experienced) are both those that accurately reflect the experience of the relationship, and ones that elevate a relationship to a highly idealized place. The death of an alcoholic spouse offers an example

that illustrates this concept. Life with an alcoholic has many negative experiences; however, in death the deceased alcoholic is often
raised to the status of sainthood. Memories in this instance may
only focus on the positive attributes of this 'wonderful' person.
Other stored symbols that reflect the misery experienced during
the deceased's lifetime are often repressed immediately following the
death. Because this expression of idealization may not match
the reality, later reality testing and cognitive restructuring of this
relationship may be a major focus of the interventions. Those who
have experienced negative relationships may not be able to produce
any positive memory, and it will be important to assist the client in
finding at least one positive memory to balance the negative
relationship.

Beginning questions can inquire about the functions provided by
this relationship and what roles were involved. Clients can also be
asked to tell the story of this relationship from the beginning.
Relationships are not just those one has with a person. They include
jobs, positions of status, and other roles one has had in a variety
of activities. Roles and relationships can be identified further by
examining some of the functions carried out by one person with
another, in relation to intimacy, guidance and assistance, companionship, nurturing, maintenance (fulfilling needs such as those for food,
clothing, shelter), and security. Thus when a client exclaims in despair
that everything has been destroyed by this loss, it is necessary to
explore each function that this lost relationship had provided in order
to determine what exactly has been lost.

Another tool that facilitates an exploration of what has been lost
is the 'psychological needs' chart (Table 2.4). This is an adaptation
of Glasser's (1990) psychological needs of love and belonging, self-
worth and self-esteem, fun, and freedom.

Used early in assessment, it asks the client how each of these
needs had been met before the loss and how they are now being met.
It is an excellent tool that visually allows the client another, and
perhaps deeper, level of understanding of his or her grief; moreover,
it reflects what a client still has in each of these areas of psychological needs that will be valuable assets in rebuilding and regaining
a sense of personal control after loss has taken away that which is
held most dear.

Illustration of psychological needs assessment
James, a 43-year-old patient, was referred to counselling after a mild
heart attack. He owned the franchise of a small business that had
suffered financially during the last year. He was accompanied by his
wife, who offered information about James that he most likely

Table 2.4 *Psychological needs*

Use as part of an assessment to understand the present situation, as it relates to the past. Example used: client who had to make major lifestyle changes following open-heart surgery.

Needs	Past	Present	Future
Affiliation Family. Friends, those I trust and can depend upon. Groups I belong to, and feel a part of; i.e. sense of belonging.	Executive – responsible for major division. Work was major group I belonged to.	Required to take a two-month leave from work.	
Power What I am in control of in my life. How are my needs for self-esteem and worth being met? Who or what validates my personal sense of competence and worth?	Total control – supervised 300 employees. Respected, admired, and often feared.	None at this time. Major loss of control of my own body – my heart has let me down.	
Fun What is my definition of fun? What do I do for fun? How much do I spend? How much do I do alone, and how much do I depend upon others	Work was fun – only social through work relationships.	Phase 1 of cardiac rehabilitation is my only social outlet. Fun at times.	
Freedom What choices do I make in terms of personal decisions, free time, how my money is spent, etc.?	Made personal decisions and decisions that affected others. Much discretionary income.	Physician now making decisions for me. Free times spent following medical orders.	

would not have revealed. Much of her information centred around his personality. He reluctantly agreed with her. She described her husband as someone who felt that what he did was never good enough. When the business had financial problems a year ago he became depressed and blamed himself, even though it was known that other franchises of this business were having the same difficulties. He was driven both personally and professionally. He compulsively watched his diet and ate only healthy foods. He exercised vigorously twice a day, and had embarked on a rigorous routine of body building. He never drank or smoked; in short, he lived life according to the most stringent rules. Presenting issues were a deep depression following a mild heart attack two months earlier, and the onset of panic attacks three weeks ago that mimicked another heart attack. Thus in addition to feelings of a deepening depression, he felt that he could not discriminate between pain caused by stress, the resulting panic attacks, and a potential new heart attack.

J: I knew I was depressed all last year because of the business. But it was nothing like I am feeling now. I can't do anything. Exercise was always my way of feeling in control. I can't even do that now.

C: Have you been restricted by your physician?

J: No, I just have no motivation, no drive. The doctor assured me that this was not serious and that exercise was important; but I just don't feel like doing anything. I keep reading books about my condition; and I can't find any reassurance that everything will be OK.

C: When it is your body and you cannot fully see what is going on internally, it's really difficult to accept your physician's statement that you will be OK and that you shouldn't worry. Sometimes it takes a while to accept what has occurred and really believe that your body will be able to function as before.

J: Yes, especially when it is your heart. My heart has failed me. I can no longer depend on it. It's not fair. I did everything right. Why didn't this happen to someone who doesn't take care of their body?

Psychologically, personality characteristics will play a major role in the treatment plan and in how much resolution can be achieved. It was ascertained that these were traits of long standing. James had always tried to make his father proud of him and never could. His father had died four years earlier, and this personal goal had never been achieved. The depression experienced three years later, following financial problems with the business, was connected to his need (but inability) to make his father proud of him. Although other franchises were having similar experiences, James had not been able to accept this decline at face value. The problems became his fault. Moreover, he lived by certain erroneous beliefs of personal control. The major distortion was the assurance of good health through personal efforts of nutrition, exercise, and living by the rules. When he perceived that his heart had failed him and that he could no longer depend upon it (without question), he withdrew from work, exercise, and outside activities with friends. As he sat at home and contemplated his demise and read medical 'stories' about cases like himself (with varying outcomes), it became only a matter of time before the onset of panic attacks that had symptoms identical to his heart attack. The relationship that had been lost was his dependence upon his body, especially his heart, to be reliable and to keep him alive.

Another goal of an initial psychological assessment is to ask the client about past experiences of a similar nature. With James it was important to know if he had ever experienced depression before the past year, and whether or not he had ever had to cope with any physical problems in the past. When asked these questions, he immediately replied that five years ago he had experienced the same feelings of deep depression for a short period of time. He had been having pain and swelling in the knee joints to the point that he had difficulty walking. Local physicians believed that a Rhesus negative factor was involved, but could not conclusively diagnose his condition. He was referred to a specialist clinic for further assessment. During the three days of testing he experienced the same feelings of depression, but chose not to tell anyone about it. The conclusions were not indicative of anything that was life-threatening, and medication was prescribed. He was instructed not to continue his exercise regime, as it could aggravate the swelling in his knees. He chose to ignore this advice, and stated that he has never had any recurrence of this condition. It became apparent that loss of physical control (through illness) was a major threat in his life, and that depression was the resulting symptom on both of these occasions. This information gleaned from the initial assessment will be the foundation on which to build interventions. It was probable that throughout sessions with James, numerous aspects of the psychological perspective would be the focal point of assessment and interventions.

Sociological

Societies and the cultures within them exert great influence on reactions to loss and ways in which their members experience grief. Multicultural issues may have to be the first issues to be addressed in an assessment in order to avoid placing the template of the dominant society over that of the client's. The culture that has shaped this client's identity and the culture that the client is living in provide a rich background for understanding this individual's unique and highly individualized grief experience. A client often feels torn between two worlds, and it is usually during a time when grief is the most acute that an individual will not feel that he or she belongs to either world.

In addition to the larger sociological understanding of a client's background and present world, it is important to assess additional sociological variables such as the individual's race, gender, socio-economic level, ethnicity, family of origin, nuclear family, and perceived support systems. Many losses are not visible and do not receive social support. Some are not understood as losses, such as the secondary ones that follow after death or another recognizable loss event. A secondary loss can be loss of a past lifestyle. Many have to move, stop leisure activities, or give up discretionary income. These are extremely difficult losses, but are often not visible. Many have commented that the funeral was not as difficult as the months and events that followed because they were numb initially, and support was available.

Questions should explore how one was socialized; what expectations were caused by gender, race, or ethnicity; how one perceives oneself in the eyes of others at this time; what ethnic or cultural rituals have helped or hindered; and what have been perceived as losses for which no social support has been received. An additional consideration is the client's status (real or perceived) in the community, work, and other activities. Social status or lack of it can be a sociological factor that exerts considerable influence on process and outcome. Those with a higher social status often have more financial means to acquire the resources needed during their bereavement period.

If the loss was a death, there are additional considerations within this perspective to assess. What was the type of death? Was it one that was validated as legitimate, or did it lack social support because a stigma was attached to it? AIDS, suicide, and murder often have issues involved that do not make them socially acceptable. These will be discussed in Chapter 7. Miscarriages and other perinatal deaths also lack social support, as potential support systems have no history with the deceased child and no memories to share about them with the bereaved parents. These deaths require the parents to grieve for a wished-for child, with little frame of reference for the relationship that was lost.

Funerals and rituals also need to be explored after a death-related loss. Questions that inquire about the type of funeral and the visiting hours often provide clues for further assessment. Some view visiting hours and the funeral rite as strong sources of emotional support; others have refused to have visiting hours and have had a closed coffin in an attempt to avoid pain. Many clients have been denied input into the planning of the funeral and this often has negative effects on their grief process. A funeral is a ritual of transition and provides the opportunity to say goodbye and begin the process of letting go. Those bereaved who choose not to be part of this type of ritual, or who are denied participation, need to find a psychologically acceptable way to begin this process.

Family and support systems can be a source of conflict or comfort. The counselling intake asks clients to indicate who lives with them now, where family members live if no longer at home, and to identify the persons who are emotionally supportive and available. Many clients lack available support systems, and this must be assessed during the early visits. Moreover, support systems may be available, but the client may not perceive them as being available when they need them, or they may be perceived as unhelpful. Time, effort, and additional grief can be lessened when the issue of support systems and a clearer understanding of them can be determined during early assessment.

Lastly, the environment as an influential factor must be considered within the framework of the sociological perspective. The environment is everything and anything; it is pervasive and ever-present. Within the business setting, the environment can be the status represented by having one's own office or secretary. The environment is whatever is a reminder that one no longer has the same title or role. Events, schedules, routines, co-workers, subordinates, activities, and objects have the potential to be painful reminders of what has been lost.

Ida was a 59-year-old female executive whose position was eliminated after restructuring had been completed at a major corporation. She had not been fired or offered an early retirement plan, and was constantly reminded by those around her that she should be grateful that she still had a job. Her salary had not changed much, but she was no longer 'head director' of a particular division. Under the new terminology of restructuring, she was labelled a 'team player', and was assured that this was a better philosophy and approach for businesses to take if they were to compete successfully in a global economy. She had fought her way up to her previous position during a time in American society that had been male-dominated at the top. She had accomplished what few women her age had been able to do; and now in one hour, it was over. She had sacrificed a marriage and family for this long-sought-after goal. She had not nurtured friendships or other systems of support during her upward climb, and now found herself alone in her crisis.

I: Every morning I come in and have to walk down the hall past my once-private office to this back room that four of us share together.

C: The grief is more than a title that has been changed. You still come to work here every day, and many rooms and items in this executive wing remind you of what has changed and what will never be the same any more.

I: Yes. And the four of us sit here and never talk about how we all feel about this. We all had similar status and titles. Now their positions have changed also, and what we do is interchangeable. By that I mean we can all do each other's job. None of us make independent decisions any more. We are all dispensable, and any one of the four of us could be eliminated if there were further budget cuts. So I guess we don't trust each other. We are not much support for each other because of our fears and lack of trust.

C: Day in and day out, that is a draining and painful situation. Is there anyone at this time that you can trust and get some support from?

This excerpt illustrates an issue of loss and grief that is becoming significant in societies that are changing and trying to adapt to the pressures and demands of a global society and economy. Sociologically speaking, economic concerns take precedence, and corporations will do what they have to do to survive. The larger human dimension does not seem to have been entered into the formula of future economic success. A loss that is related to a job or status within a workplace will be primarily around the sociological and psychological perspectives. Counsellors are trained to assess the psychological, but often overlook the subtle but influential sociological.

Physical

As the counsellor assesses this perspective, he or she must keep in mind that physical problems can create a situation of loss in and by itself that is the basis for a grief experience; that grief resulting from a physical diagnosis may raise issues that are different from other losses; and that other types of loss can bring on physical symptoms and medical problems.

Concerns with morbidity and mortality, psychosomatic symptoms, psychiatric care, medication, lack of sleep, nutrition, and general areas of functioning are all priorities for early assessment. A specific question that assesses daily functioning should also be included in the initial assessment – describe a typical day, how has your routine changed, what is difficult for you now to accomplish in a day, do you have one goal each day? – and other questions that promote a clearer understanding of the client's ability to function on a daily basis.

To illustrate this perspective, let us look at a woman with a medical diagnosis that created an intense situation of loss and grief:

Marsha was single and aged 26 when she first came to counselling following the death of her brother. She became involved in individual and group counselling, and as a result, was able to resolve many issues of grief, past and present. Many years later she volunteered at a centre for grief counselling; however, this involvement was short-lived after she had to undergo multiple surgery for 'female problems'. The final diagnosis after several operations was that she would never be able to have children. She wrote a letter that she wanted to share in order to help others understand her personal grief:

> The inability to have children after my hysterectomy two months ago really affected me on Mother's Day. Up until that time I always thought I had a choice. I did not realize that I probably did not; but I did not know this at the time because I was so sick. . . . The grief is on top of the grief I had to deal with for almost a year after being tested for ovarian cancer. . . . The other grief and depression I had to deal with was the fact that having such a serious illness was devastating my life. I could barely work, and I slept most of the time. My self-esteem took a nose-dive. It was all that I could do to get dressed in the morning. I was in a job that I was not happy with, but it was impossible at the time to change. . . . When my doctor told me that I was seriously ill, I would not believe him. He did not tell me that I had to have a hysterectomy because he feared the mental anguish that it would bring on. He allowed me to come to that conclusion on my own after I could no longer deal with the pain and disruption in my life. By that time I was willing to do anything; however, I understand that it was important that I reached this conclusion on my own.

Clients who have a physical diagnosis that creates issues of grief, or those who have physical symptoms because of a grief experience, will tend to focus on the physical perspective. This is their pain at the time and it needs to be addressed. A counsellor must be sensitive to these issues, but know when it is appropriate to change the focus. It is comfortable to centre on physical symptoms in order to avoid or circumvent the other perspectives.

History of loss

The 'History of loss' (Table 2.5) is a tool that leads the counsellor during assessment and intervention to a greater understanding of the

Table 2.5 *History of loss*

Use as part of an assessment to gain understanding of the influence of past (and often unresolved) losses on the present losses and circumstances. Client is often not aware of the past losses.

Case example: client who presented the loss of a 40-year friendship.

Loss	Age	Experiences (feelings/behaviours)	Unanswered?	What changed (money, residence, etc.)
Loss of a friendship	71	Devastated – loss of trust – depression	All unanswered in terms of what and why	Isolated self from others. Stopped all activities
Death of daughter-in-law	70	Still grieving – deep pain. Lacks support for grief	Why someone so young?	Daily life
Husband's heart attack	68	Fear and daily anxiety	None	Relationship change: overprotects him – afraid to share her issues with him
Death of sister	68	Sadness	None	
Death of sister (last sibling)	68	Worry about my own death	None	No remaining siblings. Only person remaining in family of origin
Death of father (last parent)	60	Sadness – had to sell family home	None	Change in family get-togethers

losses that a client has had to carry to this point in life. It provides a visual representation, not only of the actual losses, but also of the experience of each loss, the unanswered questions, and the changes in lifestyle experienced after each loss. Often the counsellor observes a common experience, reaction, or coping style that a client relies upon after a loss (e.g. anger, guilt, suppression), learns that a client has many unanswered questions about the losses in his or her life, or sees that there have been multiple changes following losses that there has been little control over. All of these findings provide valuable material to investigate further and for which to design intervention strategies.

Worden's tasks, Rando's Six 'R' process, and the experiences of grief

These are tools that provide a framework for an assessment when an immediate opinion regarding the status of a client is required. The 'Experiences of grief' reflects the total bereavement process. Close listening or sharing the chart (Table 2.6) will help the assessment and facilitate early joining with the client. Worden's tasks and Rando's Six 'R' process have similar functions; however, clients often report that the 'Experiences' chart seems to be more inclusive of their process of bereavement. Bereavement is not a straight, linear process; it is circular and cyclical with numerous reversions to earlier times. Using the 'Experiences', together with the chart on the 'Perspectives' (Table 2.3), provides an extended base for ongoing assessment and interventions. Working with this broader base helps avoid the risks of imposing templates of singularly defined tasks or stages on the client. Instead we join with them in their unique processes and attempt to understand them through these wider lenses.

The word 'experience' in the 'Experiences of grief' encourages an internal and external focus. *Internal* applies to emotional insight and reactions within the person, and *external* focuses on what is occurring in the environment or outside the individual's internal reality.

Grief cannot be avoided, in the truest sense of the meaning of avoidance. It is an experience that will be either ignored and repressed or actively embraced and resolved. Clients in early stages of grief express a total aloneness that first needs to be fully experienced (Experience 1) before any recognition or cognitive acceptance of the loss event can occur. This corresponds to the philosophical perspective and feelings of existential anxiety. One widow described this during her first counselling session as waking up feeling immobilized by an intense fear that took over her body. She described an incredible feeling of aloneness that resulted in sheer terror and

Table 2.6   *Experiences of grief*

1.	To experience the depths of aloneness, meaninglessness, and anxiety
2.	To experience the risk of exploration, understanding, and cognitive acceptance
3.	To fully experience all dimensions of pain: psychologically, spiritually, cognitively, emotionally, and physically
4.	To experience the present environment that is a poignant reminder of the loss
5.	To experience the risk of uncertainty: letting go, new choices
6.	To experience integration of the loss experience and to reinvest in meaningful living

panic. We believe that this is a universal experience in the early period of acute grief, and that some degree of this aloneness and anxiety must be experienced before an individual can initiate the risk of the second experience: exploration, understanding and cognitive acceptance. The term *risk* is used because grief work and the full experience of it involves the risk of additional pain. Clients will feel additional pain as they ask questions about the loss and attempt to understand what exactly has been lost and the personal impact involved. Some will try to avoid the pain of grief and not embrace this risk. Grief involves additional hurting before healing can take place. Part of the fear of additional pain lies in the reality that the loss has already occurred and that individuals feel threatened by the realization that more pain will have to be experienced in order to heal. It is difficult to comprehend the idea that the worst has already happened, and that the process of bereavement will not further destroy one.

The third experience encompasses all dimensions of pain. Thus, it is important to listen to which dimension is being embraced or avoided – the psychological, spiritual, cognitive, emotional, or physical – and then to connect with the client on that dimension. One client, who was referred by a dermatologist following the death of her husband, had experienced hair loss. Assessment, initiated by the dermatologist, indicated that this was a psychological and physiological manifestation of acute grief. This widow was avoiding the emotional expression of grief for fear of more loss of personal control. She had successfully blocked and avoided normal human emotions; however, the expression of her pain was manifested in the physical symptom of hair loss. It was necessary to help this person gain insight into her symptoms and then to provide a safe environment within the counselling sessions for emotional catharsis.

The fourth experience focuses on the need to live in the present environment that is a poignant reminder of the loss. This experience is reflective of early and middle sessions of counselling, with major influence being exerted by the psychological and sociological/cultural perspectives. Most bereaved individuals are not aware of what is meant by their environment, nor of the power it has to influence the bereavement process. Early assessment must focus on a thorough understanding of the total environment of an individual, which includes where one lives and works, daily routines, support systems, anniversaries and other special events that can trigger grief reactions. The environment is ever-present, and can often catch one unaware of the potential impact it has on the grief experience. Initially the counsellor may have to be more directive and make suggestions for alterations in the present lifestyle. For example, many try to keep all the old traditions during the holiday times, causing additional and unnecessary grief. The counsellor may find it helpful to give the client permission to change the focus of the holidays this year and to break with the old traditions. Another example of a painful environment is going to church alone. A helpful suggestion is to go to a different church of the same denomination for a while in order to maintain the benefits of attending church, yet changing to an environment of different people that would not remind one of the loss. Because the environment is ever-present, one cannot and should not try to totally avoid it. However, in order to cope with the pain of grief and regain some semblance of personal control, it is important to make small changes in everyday life. As the counselling sessions continue and the process moves from the early, acute times of grief to the middle sessions where the grief is experienced as nagging and chronic, clients will continue to focus on this experience and begin to make personal choices of change and alteration. Pain, in all its dimensions, will still be felt; however, a more active part of the process will begin that will encourage behaviours that reflect an ability to take action upon the world, and not solely to feel acted upon.

As one focuses on this experience of the environment, one is moving towards more uncertainty in terms of being in control of one's world. Although the loss has happened, and one comes to terms with the reality that what has been lost cannot be found or retrieved, there is still the psychological risk of letting go and making new choices. This is the fifth experience, and it is found more in the middle and later counselling sessions. It constitutes a major focus of the work of bereavement during this period. Assessments and interventions will continue to focus on 'letting go', and counsellors will see the continued influence of the psychological and sociological/cultural perspectives. This is not to indicate that the other perspectives are no longer emerging or exerting influence; rather, it seems as though certain perspectives have the tendency to be more prominent at different stages of the process. Again, the counsellor is cautioned not to use this as a template to impose on the client. Each person has a unique experience of grief. During this experience many will try to make new choices, but will attempt to hold on to something that is no longer there. It is possible to psychologically deceive oneself by believing that one can hold on to even a remnant of what has been lost. In Gestalt terms, we are left with unfinished business that does not allow us to make healthy new attachments in the future. Interventions must assist clients in letting go, while holding in healthy memory what has been lost.

Lastly, in later counselling sessions, the bereaved will move towards integration of the total experience of loss, which includes inter- and intrapersonal growth. Life will never be the same again; but life can be good, with purpose and meaning. Thus the sixth experience of integration and reinvestment in meaningful life will be the focus of later counselling sessions, with clients assuming more responsibility for personal change and growth. Attention to all the perspectives is important during these sessions, as they all need to be understood for their influence on the total experience: past, present, and future rebuilding of a new identity.

Psychological tests

Other assessment tools include the use of psychological tests. Some appropriate instruments include the 'Impact of events scale' (Horowitz et al., 1979), Rotter's 'Locus of control scales' (1966), the IPAT 'Anxiety questionnaire' (Cattell et al., 1957/1976), and Beck's 'Depression inventory' (1978). These tests measure psychological reactions that are common after a loss experience. They facilitate a deeper understanding of the effects that a loss event may have had upon an individual. At the same time the counsellor should be cautioned not to rely upon a psychological test as the sole tool of diagnosis, nor to use a test to pathologize an individual. Tests should only be used to arrive at a clearer understanding of an individual and his or her personal reactions and needs after an experience of loss.

3

Grief Counselling and Grief Resolution

The process of grief is an individual journey. Although losses appear to have similar qualities, and there are universal dimensions of grief, each individual has unique issues to cope with and resolve. No two people grieve in the same manner or on the same timetable. Each individual is influenced by various perspectives at different times during the process. Who comes for counselling, when, and with what issues is always idiosyncratic.

When asking the question 'who comes' for counselling, in general it appears to be those who are not able to get needed support from family or friends. This may be a result of not having family nearby, not feeling comfortable sharing deep emotions with family or friends, or the family and friends not being knowledgeable about the grief process and neglecting to provide emotional support.

Grief counselling

Bereaved clients (no matter what the loss) may request counselling at any time during the grief process. Usually, it is during a period of acute pain, frustration, or confusion regarding what to do to feel better. This can be during an early stage of the process or years removed from the actual event. Some clients come within six months after a loss, because they believe that they should be doing better or be 'over this by now'. Others come years later, and after several major losses, because they never had the time or the permission to grieve, or because the accumulation of the effects of losses has become overwhelming.

The issues that need to be addressed and resolved vary from individual to individual. Some clients simply do not understand the grief process. Thus, education is an important component of counselling. Many come from cultural backrounds which have negated the grieving process, and so they believe it to be a sign of personal weakness. Others come during a time of acute grief and want the counsellor to rescue and reassure. This can be a trap for caring mental health professionals whose mothering instincts would soothe the clients' grief. However, a major premise of grief counselling is to help clients experience the pain in order to heal, rather than to avoid or deny it. Still others come with chronic issues of grief. The acute phases may have subsided; now the issues are long-lasting ones of rebuilding new identities and making new choices.

Idiosyncrasy is also revealed in the characteristics inherent in the type of loss or the manner in which the loss occurred. If the loss was violent in nature, there may be legal complications and conflicted emotions. Often highly charged feelings, such as rage, must be addressed before the normal aspects of grief.

With regard to the counselling process for grief, there is no set number of sessions. Many come once for information about the process and validation of their grief. The majority attend between four and ten sessions during the first year after their loss. Some return a year or two later to address issues that are emerging for the first time. Most of these latter issues centre on the letting go and rebuilding phases. And, in our experience, a few clients have come weekly for as much as a year. Much depends upon the personalities, the type of loss, the coping abilities, and available support systems. Various issues may emerge at any time during the process. Some emerge more than once, but with different aspects and questions to be resolved. Other issues may never emerge and exert no influence on the client's experience. The influence that a perspective contributes to the loss experience can be positive or negative. Moreover, the influence has to be considered in terms of past and present loss(es). Examples will be given to illustrate this.

Movement from early to middle sessions of counselling is very individual and dependent upon many factors. Close listening and continued assessment provide the best guidelines as to where a client is in the process. Counselling should be a process of joining with clients on their journey and co-facilitating the experience. Professional judgement needs to be used to evaluate the effectiveness of the sessions and interventions, and to assess the client's desire and/or ability to go through this process. Those who take the risk to fully experience their grief will guide the counsellor to the next phase of their grief work.

Early sessions are marked by acute experiences of painful grief. Clients ask whether or not they will survive this experience and question if life will ever have meaning again. Pain is felt psychologically, spiritually, cognitively, emotionally, and physically. There is a feeling of total loss of control in one's life. Grief is experienced as an overwhelming assault. The middle sessions are characterized by relapses. Perspectives re-emerge that clients felt they had already addressed. They do not understand that the perspective might be the same, but the issues and aspects of it are different. The grief is chronic, nagging, and often relentless. Issues revolve around identity and role changes, and the need to create a new 'I'. Later sessions are times of rebuilding and reinvesting in meaningful life. The experience has been integrated and there is energy and motivation to make new choices. Clients initiate these sessions describing their plans, goals, and new achievements. Counselling has become a mutual experience between the client and the counsellor. According to Ivey, 'dialectics involves a search for more workable answers and a search for truth. The therapist–client relationship can also be considered a dialectical, co-constructed approach to knowledge and truth' (1986: 19).

To illustrate the above concepts, a case example will be used that highlights areas of focus during early, middle, and later counselling sessions of an individual working through his grief in the course of two years. Using the 'Perspectives' (Tables 3.1 and 3.2) and the 'Experiences of grief' (Table 2.6, p. 38) during the various sessions facilitated ongoing assessments and treatment strategies, and provided an expansion of the counsellor's awareness of the totality and depths of a client's total experience. These tools, with examples of their use, will be discussed in the following 'Case of Hank'.

The case of Hank

Hank was a 34-year-old male, married for eight years. He and his wife were building their first home, and were planning to start a family in the next year. They had carefully planned out their lives together and everything was going according to schedule. One day on the way to work, Sue was hit by a truck as she entered the expressway. She was taken to a local emergency room where she had been employed as a nurse. Despite the fact that everything possible was done by her peers, she died in the emergency room. Hank had watched for hours, and the horror of witnessing the event lasted for well over a year. He began counselling about one month after her death.

In addition to frequent flashbacks to the emergency room, Hank had to return every night to a home not yet completed. He and Sue had been doing most of the interior work to cut down on expenses. Completing the home was a major part of his grief work.

Early sessions
Counselling during the early sessions entails ongoing assessment, encouragement of expression of emotions, and the provision of needed support (non-judgmental listening). The 'Experiences of grief' (Table 2.6, p. 38) during the early sessions include (but are not limited to) the first four: (1) to experience the depths of aloneness, meaninglessness,

Table 3.1 Directions for perspectives

Considerations of perspectives	Philosophical	Spiritual	Psychological	Sociological	Physical
Early counselling sessions (acute)					
A. Contributions to present loss					
B. Contributions from past losses					
C. Interventions					
Middle counselling sessions (chronic)					
A. Contributions to present loss					
B. Contributions from past losses					
C. Interventions					

Later counselling
sessions (reinvesting
and rebuilding)

A. Contributions to
   present loss

B. Contributions
   from past losses

C. Interventions

Perspectives: Tool for assessment and intervention. They can exert a positive or a negative influence at any time during the experience of grief. They may also be absent or exert no influence. They may emerge differently at different times, presenting different issues.

Directions:

1. Assess where the client is in the counselling process (early, middle, later).
2. Listen for characteristics of the various perspectives which are exerting an influence.
3. Make notes on the chart that indicate where a client is at in the process (time) and perspective(s). These can be direct quotes, or your reflections of the content or observations of nonverbals.
4. As perspectives are noted, explore for past losses and possible influences (positive and negative) that each perspective might have exerted. Make notes.
5. Review chart after assessment(s) and ongoing sessions. Design interventions based on where the client is at (time frame) and current influence of perspectives.

Table 3.2 *Case example using perspectives*

Considerations of perspectives	Philosophical	Spiritual	Psychological	Sociological	Physical
	(Some perspectives have or exert a positive influence and others have negative influences over the entire process)				
Early counselling sessions (acute)					
A. Contributions to present loss	Cannot tolerate being alone. 'I don't feel like I am living in my body.' Reflects many existential anxieties.	Never attended church/no personal relationship with God or a higher being.	Deep emotional pain. Reliving memories of the ER. Suicidal ideation. Pre-morbid personality of dependency. Sees self as hopeless and useless.	'My friends are good support systems.' Presently living with a friend because the environment of his home is too painful.	Nct able to sleep. Minimal daily functioning. Multiple symptoms of depression.
B. Contributions from past losses	At the present time, Jim is not aware of any past losses in his life that might be exerting an influence on the present.				
C. Interventions	Listen – reflection – Verbal tracking – validate the pain.	Not addressed at this time – does not appear to be exerting any influence.	Encourage repetition of story in order to release pain. Facilitate a contract to not commit suicide.	Encourage return to environment as tolerated in order to relive the memories to initiate the emotional release.	Explore dietary and sleep patterns. Encourage medical involvement for evaluation.

Middle counselling sessions (chronic)

A. Contributions to present loss	Expresses desire to meet others 'like him' to see if their experiences are similar.	Deceased wife was Catholic. Attended a Mass for the dead in her memory. Became upset during the Mass and was also upset at the concept of this type of religious service.	Reviews marital relationship and issues of dependency. Feels full range of emotions.	'My friends don't call me any more.' Address cultural issues of men and grief.	Continues to have sleep difficulties. Explores options for an exercise programme. Begins walking and scuba diving.
B. Contributions from past losses	No prior loss of this type or experience with this perspective.	No prior experience.	Becomes aware of past (unnoticed) relationship losses with wife and parents.	Aware of past cultural scripts. Aware of past negative relationship with father.	No past experience.
C. Interventions	Joined support group – met other widowed people his age.	Arranged a meeting with a priest to explain the 'ritual' and meaning of this Mass/Catholic tradition.	Continue to facilitate expressions of painful grief. Explore personal issues to gain insight. Address faulty cognitions.	Encourage ritual of inviting friends over to commemorate together. Experience pain of environment.	Encourage physical activities. Continue medications as prescribed by physician.

continued overleaf

Table 3.2   *(Continued)*

Considerations of perspectives	Philosophical	Spiritual	Psychological	Sociological	Physical
(Some perspectives have or exert a positive influence and others have negative influences over the entire process)					
Later counselling sessions (reinvesting and rebuilding)					
A. Contributions to present loss	Discuss grief experience in relation to growth that has transpired.	Tried a 'church' – liked the friendliness and the caring of the people.	Address ways to rebuild a new identity. More cognitive awareness of past faulty assumptions and beliefs.	Questions continue re: influence of socialization, norms, etc. Reflections back to childhood.	Decrease in physical symptoms. Ongoing exercise programme.
B. Contributions from past losses	No prior experience.	No prior experience.	Use 'History of loss' to gain insight into past losses.	Impact of early socialization.	No previous experience.
C. Interventions	Encourage integration and transpersonal growth and self-actualization.	Encourage continued exploration of spirituality.	Use psychological needs chart for ongoing assessments and strategy planning.	Promote adjustments to new choices and readjustment to environment.	Encourage maintenance of physical programme.

and anxiety; (2) to experience the risk of exploration, understanding, and cognitive acceptance; (3) to fully experience all dimensions of pain: psychologically, spiritually, cognitively, emotionally, and physically; and (4) to experience the present environment that is a poignant reminder of the loss. During the acute experiences of grief, clients initially experience an incredible sense of aloneness and meaninglessness. Many describe this time as feeling as if they are outside of their bodies, looking in. Others experience tremendous anxiety, to the point of panic. Spiritually, they ask why God has allowed this to happen to them; and psychologically, they are 'searching for what has been lost'. This search reflects the fact that the psyche has not been able to accept the reality of the loss and tries to undo it by retrieving it. This often occurs in the form of clients mentally replaying the event, looking for different endings; dreaming of what has been lost; or hearing and seeing the lost object in a crowd. Sociologically, during the early sessions, support systems or lack of them will be identified; and influences such as gender and ethnicity will be most apparent. Lastly, physical perspectives often focus on psychosomatic complaints and difficulties with eating and sleeping. These perspectives and their influence have been discussed in Chapters 1 and 2.

Along with continued assessment and early interventions, questions can be directed towards exploring the possible contributions to the present loss from these various perspectives. This can provide insight into the personal meaning of the loss for the bereaved, the nature and the meaning of the attachment (relationship) to the deceased (or the 'object' that has been lost), how much of the self (identity) has been lost, what personality factors are involved, what are the main issues that need to be addressed, what are the primary emotions of the bereaved, and what has changed in their lives as a result of the loss. These questions are not all-inclusive, but they do provide a framework for early exploration.

The early assessment and interventions with Hank focused on gaining an understanding of the relationship that he had with his wife, the functions provided by that relationship, and a general understanding of Hank's personality and his pre-morbid functioning.

Hank was the passive person in the relationship. On a daily basis, Sue usually made the decisions and followed through on them. On a larger scale, she had chosen the plan for the house and had decided on the interior design. There was nothing in that home that was not a part of her and there was nothing in Hank's day-to-day functioning that was not a reminder of the loss. Her death paralysed him. Other than going to work, he could barely function on his own.

   H: I just can't sleep in that house. I tried sleeping in the extra
       bedroom and then a chair. Sue is all over that house. I can't
       stand being there alone. I'm staying with friends now. I don't
       know if I will ever be able to sleep in that house again.
   C: It sounds like you are being overwhelmed by too many
       memories.
   H: Yes. I really can't stand this pain. My friends made me sign
       this agreement not to hurt myself. I did, but I'm not sure if I
       can stick to it. I have never experienced much loss in my life;
       but I have never felt this way, and I don't feel like I am living
       in my own body.
   C: You hurt so much right now and nothing seems to take away
       the pain. Suicide seems like a good choice to stop the agony.
   H: Yes. But my friends are good support systems. Jane sits up
       with me and talks me through these feelings and thoughts until
       I can go to sleep. Somehow I have gotten through these last
       three weeks since the funeral. I had to be held up to walk
       down the aisle at the funeral. I couldn't have done it without
       all my friends. I was so used to Sue doing everything that I
       have to rely on my friends now. I'm useless and helpless.

The above excerpt reflects the experience of the depths of aloneness, meaninglessness, and anxiety; the experience of all the dimensions of pain; and the experience of the environment that was causing
additional pain. The philosophical, psychological, sociological, and
physical perspectives were exerting the most influence during these
early sessions. Currently, Hank was not aware of any past losses;
therefore, he was not able to understand how past experiences (positive or negative) affect present emotions. The sociological perspective, in terms of reliable support systems, was the most positive
perspective, whereas the other mentioned perspectives contributed
more difficult aspects to address.

   During early sessions, encourage clients to tell the story of what
happened. Encourage details and provide opportunity for expressions of grief as they relate their stories. This is a good opportunity
to assess whether they have the correct information, lack a clear
understanding of what transpired, or for some reason cannot talk
about the event or person. The more they talk, the more the cognitive acceptance is integrated. Psychologically, to accept the reality
that this death (or loss event) has occurred, asking questions and
encouraging repetition of the stories promotes integration of the
event and eventual acceptance. By talking, and as the loss is cognitively accepted, feelings will emerge. The more feelings that they can
release, the more capable they are of moving forward in their grief

work. Family and friends are often immersed in their own grief, so that they may fail to be supportive of the emotional experience of the bereaved client. Counsellors also need to assess the type of support that is coming from these systems. Support systems may be hindering a normal grief process if they are helping the bereaved avoid their grief. Moreover, many who form the support systems lack information about normal grief and try to rush the process. Examples of this are family and friends who encourage the bereaved to dispose of the clothing and memorabilia the day after the funeral, or who keep the bereaved person so busy that he or she has no time to think.

A primary benefit of counselling is that it provides an environment conducive to releasing these intense emotions. Counsellors need to be aware of the intensity of emotions being expressed. Sessions may have to run longer if clients are still experiencing intensity and have not returned to some level of stability. It would not be responsible to release a client to drive home who had just got in touch with a high level of anger. Probe for feelings early in a session in order to allow time for both expression and a return to some state of equilibrium. The following exchange was initiated within the first ten minutes of a session, and it required a full session to process the total experience. The client needed to share it, relive it, and become emotionally stabilized before leaving. Grief work is hard work and takes time. Do not rush the process.

C: I know this is difficult, but I do not know all that happened that day. Can you tell me more about it?

H: [*Crying*] She was coming on to Route 30. It's never been a good entry. A lot of us have complained about it, but no one has ever done anything to fix the curve that makes a blind spot. It was raining, and that made it even harder to see. I don't know if she didn't see the truck coming, or if she thought she could accelerate and get on. He [the trucker] said he didn't see her until it was too late.

C: How did you find out about it?

H: I was on my way to work. I usually leave twenty minutes after she did. I saw the ambulances, then I saw Sue's car.

C: What a nightmare, to stop and see your wife's car.

H: I froze. I just couldn't believe it. I don't know how long I stood there.

C: You must have felt that this was a bad dream. It couldn't have felt like it was really happening to you.

H: Yeah. But then a friend came along. We all grew up together down here and we all married school friends and live here still.

> Many of us travel the same roads every day. She took me to
> the hospital. I don't even remember the ride. But I'll never
> forget those hours in the emergency room. [*Sobbing at this
> point*] Maybe if I had been more aware of what was going on I
> would have insisted that we had taken her to a trauma centre.
> Maybe she would have lived. Why couldn't I have insisted on
> this? I wouldn't be going through this now if I had.

Feelings of unreality and numbness, with intrusions of intense
pain, are hallmarks of initial grief experiences. Psychologically, we
are not ready for these assaults and do not immediately comprehend
or process them. The early sessions of grief counselling also need to
address regrets and feelings that something different could have been
done by the survivors that would have changed the course of events.
This is a normal part of the process whereby the bereaved need to
replay the event, search for what has been lost, and work through
feelings of guilt and anguish that they were not able to prevent the
event.

Gradually over time, with release of emotion, permission to go
back over events and feelings, and provision of a supportive environment, the bereaved will experience a lessening of the acute
intensity of pain. They will realize that they are beginning to
experience days with segments of time that are not painful. Hope
begins to build on this new experience of freedom from pain for
short periods of time. Clients are encouraged to keep journals on a
daily basis in order to gain awareness of what is changing and
happening within them and in their environment.

During the latter part of the early sessions, counsellors introduce
the idea that grief work is multidimensional and that there is more
to grieve than just an individual; there are also all the objects and
associations connected with that individual. Counsellors, from listening over a number of sessions, now have some understanding of their
clients' worlds and all that needs to be grieved (from 'we to I', to
lifestyle changes, to treasured objects that connected individuals to
relationships). Grieving important objects or places eventually allows
the bereaved to let go of the past connections and reframe them into
new meanings. An example of this is a favourite chair that belonged
to the deceased. Initially the chair is a source of pain. Gradually that
chair has to be grieved and a decision made about it. For example,
some might decide to give it to a family member who sees it as a
comforting reminder of the deceased; others may decide that there is
no more emotional connection to it and give it to a charity; still
others may reframe the meaning of the chair from painful memories
to peaceful connections. In the event that the chair can become a

place of solace, one can then sit and feel close in memory to that which has been lost.

> *H*: I'm beginning to understand this grief business. I'm doing what you suggested. Last night I went to the restaurant where we ate every week and sat in the same place and grieved that. I made myself sit there and do it. I felt better after that. Now I know that there's a lot of places that I have to go to. I had been avoiding them because it hurt too much. But I've been trying what you have told me, and you haven't lied to me about anything.

The counselling process begins to move towards the middle sessions at this point.

Middle sessions

During the middle parts of the counselling process, practitioners will hear reflections of continued pain and the torment of adjusting to and grieving an environment that is a poignant reminder of the loss (see Table 2.6, numbers 1–4, p. 38). During the latter period of these middle sessions, clients begin to be willing to experience the risk of uncertainty: letting go and making new choices (number 5). Once past the acute phases, where more emotional support is necessary, bereaved individuals move into new realms that need exploration and intervention. Perspectives emerge and re-emerge, often centring on the psychological and sociological ones. Psychologically, the bereaved feel more in control of their emotions. They have begun to make new decisions and take small risks in an effort to rebuild their lives. From a sociological perspective, they gain understanding of the influence of their cultural backgrounds and often discard some of the negative messages that had previously influenced them. An example of this is the fact that men in white, middle-class society are often socialized not to have emotions. Moreover, many Americans and Britons have been indoctrinated with the belief that expressing grief is a sign of weakness. Philosophically, many bereaved clients have found support from other bereaved individuals and no longer experience existential aloneness and meaninglessness. Spiritual perspectives often arise during this time, even for those who have not had a spiritual background. Many begin to question an afterlife and wonder where their loved one is. Some will talk to a clergy-person and ask questions about spiritual issues. Lastly, physical perspectives can continue to exert influence and create additional stress during this time. Hank could not sleep, was unable to eat, and lost significant weight. Much of his grief was being expressed through physical symptoms.

During these middle sessions it is important to assess prior losses as they pertain to and influence the perspectives (see Table 3.2, p. 46). Prior losses are assessed through the 'History of loss' which is introduced (at least verbally) during the intake. The use of the chart on 'Perspectives' facilitates questioning into past losses and how possible contributions (from the past) might be affecting the present loss. For example, for a person who has experienced a major loss in the past and has healed because of his or her spirituality, it is quite possible for this past experience to exert positive influence in the present loss. This tool offers a basis for investigation and treatment planning. During these middle sessions, counsellors should explore each perspective and build treatment plans on the findings.

> *H*: [*four months later*] My friends don't call very much any more and if they stop by, they won't come in. They have to hurt too. Sue was their friend also. We all grew up together. I know this and I feel bad for them, but this doesn't help me. I'm back home now. I've survived that, but this house is too big and I still haven't put any of Sue's things away. I still have days when I don't know if I can make it, or even care.
>
> *C*: You understand their pain; however, you feel a sense of abandonment. I'm also thinking that as time goes on, you are becoming socially isolated and you are not sure how to connect with your friends. You don't want to cause them more pain, but you need their support still. The support you need from them now may be different than what you needed two months ago. It sounds like you are not certain what you need or how to ask for it.
>
> *H*: That's right. Two months ago I couldn't do a thing. My friends had to take over my life for me. Maybe I drained them and they've had enough. I still think we all need to grieve together, and we really haven't done that because I was so needy then.
>
> *C*: One way of grieving together is to share favourite memories. You all knew her differently, and part of grieving and healing is to remember this person who had a beginning and middle to her life; not just an end. Why not use this handout on 'Reminiscing' [Table 3.3] as a starting place and ask your friends to think about their memories and come together at your home to share them.

Hank agreed to this. He wrote invitations to his friends and included the handout. They all came and shared. The gathering lasted four hours, with many positive outcomes. Friends came together and began

Table 3.3   *Reminiscing*

In addition to sharing pictures, items, and favourite stories about your loved one, the following questions offer an opportunity for personal reflections and sharing about the meaning and purpose of a loved one's life.

What will you never forget about _____ ?

What did you like most about _____ ?

What was unusual or out of character for _____ ?

What was the favourite expression of _____ ?

What was a favourite song or type of music of _____ ?

What was _____ favourite way of doing things?

What qualities of _____ would you like to have?

What do you hope that others will always remember about _____ ?

If _____ were face to face with you now, what would you say or do?

How would you describe _____ to a stranger?

---

a new chapter in their lives. Support for each other was renewed and understood in different dimensions. Another important outcome was that the house itself was grieved and a new identity for the house began that day. Many had been avoiding Hank because they were avoiding memories of Sue in that place.

Towards the latter part of the middle sessions the bereaved become more aware of the necessity to leave behind former identities and to begin the search for new aspects of themselves that have not yet emerged. Sessions will move from emphasis on expressing painful emotions to making new choices. Counsellors facilitate this transition by assisting clients in decision-making and exploring new options in their lives. We cannot change what has happened, and eventually clients need to adapt and move beyond grief. The ability to make decisions reawakens personal feelings of being in control. Loss and grief remove feelings of control. Counselling must address regaining control both within individuals and in their environments. Attig (1992) terms this task *relearning the world*. The bereaved are no longer the same and cannot try to live in their worlds as they once did. All have some potential to relearn and live life differently, yet meaningfully. Counselling has the potential to offer a major contribution in this regard.

H: I realize that I have to find some new activities. Tom doesn't ask me to go trap shooting on Friday night any more because that would leave his wife alone. Sue and Tanya used to do things together on these nights.

C: You seem to be realizing that even though these will always be close friends, some things will never be the same again and that you have to find new things to do that don't include them.

H: Yes. You know the people I stayed with for the month after Sue died? Well, they were not part of this group of friends that I had grown up with. Sue had worked with them in the hospital, and I had never met them until she died. Well, they enjoy scuba diving. The local YMCA is offering classes, and I thought that I would sign up. I just have to do something different, and I have to fill up some of the empty spaces.

C: That sounds like a great idea; I never would have come up with that.

Later sessions

Later sessions do not declare that grief work has ended completely. There is no one right way to grieve and there is no set timetable for the specific experiences. There is some agreement in the field that at least two years is needed. However, even this time can vary, depending upon the loss; and this does not mean that counselling is needed for two years. Some may need only one professional visit, but will, on their own, take a full two years to experience their grief and begin to rebuild their lives. The basic guideline for assessment and treatment is to be aware of potential problems associated with personalities, pre-morbid functioning, and complications after loss; but to reserve judgement on an individual's manner of grieving and the amount of time he or she takes to go through the process.

A major part of these later sessions addresses the experience of letting go and making new choices and the experience of integration and reinvestment (see Table 2.6, numbers 5 and 6, p. 38). Reinvestment does not mean replacement. Simply stated, it is the willingness and the ability to invest mental and emotional energy in the business of living a meaningful life. Since grief is considered to be a cyclical process, it is possible for many of the earlier experiences to re-emerge, in much the same way as the perspectives do. Often holidays, anniversary dates, and other special events trigger emotions and create reversion to earlier experiences. The perspectives will indicate a process of integration of the loss and signs of future growth. Philosophically, the bereaved find meaning and purpose again in life. They feel connected to others and a larger system beyond themselves. They are aware that life is not fair, but they can appreciate the goodness of it. Spiritually, many who have been angry at God have seen past their anger and have re-established their relationship with God or a higher being. Many experience growth in their spirituality and realize that even as adults they may have had childish views and expectations of God. Psychologically, they have made many new decisions and choices and understand the concepts of role realignment and new identities. Many have had to change their belief systems and accept new ways of thinking, such as the reality that bad things do happen to good people. During these final sessions an adaptation of Glasser's (1990) psychological needs (Table 3.4) can provide a framework for exploration and rebuilding based upon specific needs. This is a worksheet, discussed in Chapter 2 as an assessment tool, that identifies basic needs of love, belonging, self-worth, fun, and freedom. Clients identify how these needs were met in the past, what has changed in the present, and possible steps to take to meet these needs again. In a graphic way, it facilitates awareness of changes that have occurred because of loss, and encourages the search for new choices that will satisfy each need. New goals should be simple, realistic, concrete, and attainable in the near future. Longer-term goals can be set once there is a firmer foundation to build upon.

From a sociological perspective, many have new-found friends, new activities, and new support systems. Environments have changed somewhat, so the former ones no longer have the potential to exert such painful influence. Many have had to rethink their cultural backgrounds and accept different ways of coping with their grief. Some men have joined with their wives in counselling to be supportive, and later acknowledge (sheepishly) that they are there for themselves also. Many have been raised in families that are very stoic, where grief is seen as selfish or a sign of weakness.

Finally, from a physical perspective during the later sessions, symptoms diminish that aggravated the grief during the early and middle sessions. Clients' outward appearances change. Some walk with a livelier pace and appear to have had a heavy weight removed from their shoulders. Others have become involved in exercise routines and tell you how much better they feel, and others laugh and show a renewed interest in life.

> H: [*nine months later*] After inquiring into scuba diving, I didn't want to do it. I went back and forth; I couldn't make up my mind what to do. Then it was too late and I had to wait until the next time it was offered. Almost nine months have gone by, but I've finally joined the local YMCA and have taken up scuba diving. It's with a new group of people, doing something

Table 3.4　*Instructions for psychological needs*

Needs	Past	Present	Future
Love: Those whom I can trust and love me, and I can love in return (family, friends, etc.).			
Belonging: List what you belong to/what you feel comfortable with/feel a part of and contribute to.			
Worth: What do I do or like about myself, that makes me feel good about myself?			
Recognition: Who appreciates me and gives me recognition? What do I do that I feel is worthwhile and important to me?			
Fun: What did I do for fun – alone/with others? How much does it cost? How much of my fun is free?			
Freedom: What does freedom mean to me? Time, money, what I eat, activities, choices, what I say.			

Directions:
1. Instruct clients to fill out how each need was met before the change (loss), illness, or death.
2. Write down (present) how these same needs are being met, or not being met, have changed or have been compromised in some way.
3. Facilitate clients to think about new ways/choices to meet these needs in the near future. Encourage small, attainable, realistic goals.

totally different. I also get a lot of exercise from this and that feels good. I like the excitement from it. Last week the group went up to Lake Erie and did some night diving around old wrecked ships. Next month we will go to a place in upstate New York. I feel like I'm 'living on the edge' doing these things. It's pretty safe, yet there is an element of danger. I have lived through the worst with Sue's death and I can never go back to the way life was then. It was almost boring. It was so predictable. I always let Sue decide everything. Doing things like this now are my choice, and I'm enjoying them. I never knew about things like scuba diving. I feel like I need challenges now.

H: [*15 months later*] Well, I finally have things completed both inside and outside of the house. There were times when I never thought I could do even one area. This weekend I finished the deck. Some friends came over to help and we made a day of it. I also bought a computer and have wired my house into it for different functions. I just read the instructions and figured how to put it together and operate it. You know this is all really good, but I'm still lonely and I don't like it. This is another hard part that you told me about. I wish I knew when this would end.

H: [*18 months later*] I'm really doing well with this computer. People are asking me to install systems in their homes. I have mine talking, answering the phone, turning on lights and other things like that. I never went to college, but I'm pretty good at things like this. It just sort of comes natural. Since high school all I ever did was to repair lawnmowers, and that always seemed good enough. I had an appointment to go to Annapolis, but didn't pass the eye exam. So I just stayed here and married Sue. We had part of my grandfather's farm to build this home on and that always seemed good enough.

About three years after his wife's death, Hank remarried and had begun to develop his own computer (service) business. Counselling did not fix his grief; however, it provided a secure environment and the education to experience and process the acute and extended phases of grief. Through counselling, this individual was able to move from dependency and passivity and be transformed through his grief into a healthier and more assertive, secure individual. He dared to endure the pain and to trust in the counselling process. He took risks to become a different person. The individual who did not have the strength to walk down the aisle alone for his wife's funeral found the resources and made the commitment to fully experience his grief.

Resolution and growth

Within the broader considerations of resolution there is an understanding and an acceptance that life will never be the same again and that certain realities and assumptions must be relinquished in order to survive the pain, to integrate the experience, and to rebuild a future existence. Resolution, like reinvestment, is not replacement. This notion may be difficult for a client to comprehend. Many modern societies are based upon the replacement of objects and relationships. Often grief counselling must address current philosophies of the society/culture of the bereaved. Nothing, whether it was a relationship or an activity (e.g. a job), that was lost is ever replaced. A meaningful part of an identity and investment of time is never replaced; it is reorganized after grief and incorporated in memory in a manner that has potential to console and be growth-producing. That which has been lost is integrated within, and is always a part of the human spirit. Grief has the potential to be a growth experience.

Along with the above considerations regarding resolution, the question is often asked: 'When is grief work ended?' This question cannot be clearly or definitively answered. Individual timetables, anniversary reactions, personality, and the influence of various perspectives are some of the factors that make it a unique experience for each individual. Moreover, the concept of ended grief work implies that the grief will never again have to be addressed. Grief resolution seems to be a more accurate term and complements the concept of grief as a process. However, even considering a broader view, there is no accepted concept of grief resolution. The differences of opinion are in terms of what resolution is and what it is not. Some believe resolution means getting over the loss and forgetting. Others believe that one never entirely gets over a loss; rather, the larger process is to learn to cope, live with it, and integrate that which has been lost in healthy memory. The following illustrates the grief work, process, and resolution of one client.

A middle-aged widow had never worked outside her home. She and her husband had raised four children, who had left home and were independent. Both looked forward to this new period in their lives. The dream was short-lived after the husband was diagnosed with cancer of the liver. For eight months they tried every available treatment, including unendorsed treatments outside the country. He died within a year of his first diagnosis. He had been her whole life. She had no identity separate from him. For some time after his death, nothing brought solace. The pleasant memories caused the most pain. He had owned his own business which she was being encouraged to sell quickly. Because of her deep pain, she could not attend to this business matter. After her husband had been deceased about six months, she began to attend a support group. Here she met four other widows around her age. Together, this small group of women worked their way through the grief process, helping each other to share similar memories. At some point after her first year of bereavement, encouraged by her new friends, she decided to run the business herself. Seven years later, she was successful and had expanded the business. The memory of her husband was alive within her and was a positive force that has allowed her to tap hidden potential. His memory will never be forgotten; the company that he started lives on through his wife.

Grief holds the possibility of tremendous growth. However, it is premature to mention this during early sessions. In the early and middle sessions clients primarily need a trusting environment that validates their normal grief reactions. In the latter part of the middle sessions and the later sessions, cautiously (and on the clients' timetables) move them towards new choices and the viewpoint that grief not only has a negative value, but it can also be a challenge and an opportunity.

The pain, experience, and resolution of grief takes place on two levels: within oneself and within one's environment. It involves many changes and reflects many dimensions. How the world has previously been viewed and various personal belief systems may need revision. Many have been raised according to certain religious, philosophical, and ethical principles. The art of counselling involves becoming involved in existential crises: e.g., 'I have been a good person and this is not fair. Is anything worth it?' The world can be a cruel place, and life is not fair; but counselling can assist the client through this crisis. What does a client have left after this experience of loss? Resolution entails making an assessment of psychological needs, evaluating what is still intact, and determining how life can be rebuilt. Resolution involves a process of acting upon the world again, making decisions, and choosing effective behaviours. It can be compared to learning how to walk again: take small steps, consistently; fall, get up, and try again. Resolution is a choice, but it may be the hardest task individuals have to face. It also involves hope and a belief that life will get better and that the pain will subside. Without this, it is difficult to set goals, to trust, to take risks.

Resolution does not mean forgetting. Some may tenaciously hold on to their grief for fear of forgetting a relationship that was so much a part of their lives. The more that others tell the bereaved to stop talking and to continue with their lives, the more the process is retarded. Resolution does mean making new choices; thus, to talk about nothing else or to grieve without breaks is not healthy either. Resolution implies an eventual letting go; more importantly, it necessitates an integration in healthy memory.

4

Family Grief

This chapter discusses various aspects of family grief, with consideration of issues that will be different for each family member. It will illustrate family case examples, but will also ask the reader to keep the individual in mind as a separate entity since most counsellors see clients individually (independent of the family unit) and their bereavement is addressed within that individual context.

Every client represents and is influenced by membership of one or more families. These memberships need to be assessed and understood as one deals with the individual. Much attention has been given to the family, especially during these times of change as we approach a new century. The family as a system has been well researched and discussed. From a systemic view, the family is understood as an 'entity maintained by the mutual interaction of its parts' (Davidson, 1983: 26). What happens in one part will affect the others. Although patterns in families are undergoing change, Zimmerman (1992) proposes that the fundamental concept of family is that it represents distinct types of close relationships that continue to have meaning and value for the individual and for larger society. The family historically has provided the framework of a fundamental social unit that produces and raises children, cares for the elderly and the disabled, and socializes its members in the basic values of individual character development and in general responsibilities of citizenship (Wisensale, 1992). Sprenkle and Piercy, considering the current influence of constructivism upon postmodern thought, proposed the following as a criterion for a healthy family:

> a healthy family is a kinship group whose primary functions include providing for the physical well-being of its members, the nurturing socialization of children, and the meeting of basic emotional needs for unconditional love. . . . Families should empower persons to become capable of living both loving and productive lives. Family members should relate to one another in ways that are nonexploitive and encourage a similar attitude toward the broader community. Family values should include the belief that all humans have equal opportunity regardless of gender, race, creed, sexual preferences, or age (independent of maturity and training). (1992: 406)

This definition allows one to consider a variety of different types of family and to understand an individual in the context of the unique type of family membership that has shaped and influenced his or her identity. Many societies propose two parents and their children as the norm for the definition of family. Today many societies are acknowledging different configurations of 'family': one-parent families with children, couples without children, blended families from remarriages, grandparents parenting children, and couples of the same sex raising children are all current examples.

When working with individuals or families some background in family theory and therapy will provide important guidelines for assessment and interventions.

Basic family tasks

Within every culture there are basic, prescribed tasks that are essential for every family to perform. When these tasks are not adequately performed, societies intervene. Duvall and Miller (1985) outline eight tasks expected by the American family. Among them are: the provision of food, clothing, and shelter; the determination of who provides the care, support, and management of the home; the establishment of ways to communicate, interact, and express affection, aggression, and sexuality; and the maintenance of morale and motivation, reward and achievement, meeting personal and family crises, setting and attaining goals, and developing family loyalties and values. The absence of any one of these, or the other four tasks, could constitute a loss in itself; and certainly when individuals present issues of loss in counselling, these basic tasks of a family (or tasks unique to a particular culture) must be taken into consideration in assessment.

An example of this was an ethnic family of three generations who came for counselling following the murder of an adolescent girl by a boyfriend from another race and culture. Besides her death, there were other losses past and present in this family's history. Included as a loss was the belief held by the grandparents that the family had been shamed, and there was a loss of family loyalties and values. They firmly believed that one should not develop intimate relationships outside one's own race. In their eyes their granddaughter had already been lost; moreover, she had been disloyal by having disregarded deep-seated family values. The parents of the deceased girl felt that they had failed as parents in their basic roles of providing care and establishing effective communication with their daughter. Their expectations of parental roles and the demands of their particular culture had to be understood and addressed, along with the obvious issues of current grief.

Family development tasks

In addition to some basic family tasks, developmental tasks within a family, or stages of the family life cycle (Table 4.1), must also be considered. Duvall and Miller (1985) refer to these tasks as being relative to a given stage of development in the life-cycle of a family. When counselling a family it is important to assess where each member is in his or her individual stage of development and where the family (in which they currently hold membership) is. Even if the family is not seen in counselling as a group (i.e. the client comes for individual counselling), this does not negate the importance of assessing the individual's family's stage of development. These tasks have been defined as growth responses that arise at certain stages in the life of the family, 'the successful achievement of which leads to present satisfaction, approval, and success with later tasks; whereas failure leads to unhappiness in the family, disapproval by society, and difficulty with later family tasks' (Duvall & Miller, 1985: 47). From this it becomes understandable that every individual has the potential to be working on more than one issue simultaneously. An individual who requests counselling for a specific loss event, which he or she believes is unrelated to any other facet of his or her life, may not be aware of unresolved family developmental tasks (past or present) that are contributing to the present loss event. The eight stages, as outlined in Table 4.1, range from the newly married couple, through the age-related tasks of caring for children, through middle age, ending with tasks that face ageing family members and their families. This model, no doubt, will need revision to accommodate new and changing definitions of the family; however, every model will include a beginning stage of basic family organization, and move towards middle age and ageing-related tasks. Whether or not all future families will include children does not preclude the concepts of a life-cycle or tasks. When a major loss such as death, divorce, or chronic illness occurs unexpectedly during a critical period of a family developmental task, it is often doubtful that effective coping, attention to the family developmental task and individuals' developmental tasks, and healthy resolution of each member's issues of bereavement can be accomplished satisfactorily without support, education, and specific therapeutic interventions.

Family concepts within the family therapy approach

Not every family, or individual within a family, will need counselling; however, an understanding of the major theoretical concepts of family will prove valuable in the counsellor's general understanding

Table 4.1   *Stage-sensitive family developmental tasks through the family life-cycle*

Stage of the family life-cycle	Positions in the family	Stage-sensitive family developmental tasks
1. Married couple	Wife Husband	Establishing marital dyad
2. Childbearing	Wife-mother Husband-father Infant daughter or son or both	Rearing tasks
3. Pre-school age	Wife-mother Husband-father Daughter-sister Son-brother	Adapt to needs of pre-schoolers
4. School age	Wife-mother Husband-father Daughter-sister Son-brother	Adapting to the community of school-age families
5. Teenage	Wife-mother Husband-father Daughter-sister Son-brother	(a) Balancing freedom and responsibility (b) Establishing post-parental interests
6. Launching centre	Wife-mother-grandmother Husband-father-grandfather Daughter-sister-aunt Son-brother-uncle	(a) Rituals for young adults leaving (b) Maintaining a supportive base
7. Middle-aged parents	Wife-mother-grandmother Husband-father-grandfather	(a) Refocus on marital dyad (b) Ties with older and younger generations
8. Ageing family members	Widow or widower Wife-mother-grandmother Husband-father-grandfather	Coping with endings and transitions

Source: adapted from Duvall, 1985, p. 62.

of the relationship of an individual within a family or families to concepts of bereavement. Family therapy has incorporated theory from various disciplines, including concepts from communications and systems theories, strategic and structural approaches, and constructivism. All of these offer insights and tools for assessments and interventions, and can be adapted to counselling for those experiencing loss and grief.

Communications and systems theories

Communications theory includes concepts from cybernetics and general systems theory. This theory encourages exploration of patterns of communication within a family setting in order to assess present behaviours and issues. Messages sent between family members are said to have report (content) and command (defining relationships) functions. Jackson (1965) observed that one can discern what the family rules are by listening to the report and command functions and the regularity of these types of family message. These rules have the primary purpose of maintaining family homeostasis or balance. Homeostasis can be further understood by using concepts from general systems theory, which has promoted the idea that a system is more than the aggregate of its parts. In terms of family therapy, this concept has been adapted to propose that a family system should be viewed as more than a collection of people, and that therapists should investigate what is helping to maintain the system. Symptoms are often considered to be mechanisms that maintain a dysfunctional system. Homeostasis (as a self-regulatory mechanism), involving positive and negative feedback loops, is a central principle in this theory, as it was in the theory of cybernetics. Nichols and Schwartz (1991) discussed the relationship of positive and negative feedback loops, family rules, and homeostasis to family therapy. The rules, both spoken and unspoken, that govern family behaviours are regulated by the need for a family to keep things in balance and control. This balance can be good for family functioning and survival; however, taken to an extreme it can become rigid. Negative feedback helps enforce the rules and minimize change in behaviour, whereas positive feedback allows or promotes change. Both of these feedback loops have a place in the overall functioning of a family, and both need to be evaluated at any given time for their potential deleterious effects on normal functioning. This model does not attempt to discover what the real problem is; the main focus is on the system as the problem and how it is being maintained.

A leader in family systems therapy was Murray Bowen (1974) who based his theoretical-clinical model on psychoanalytical theory and practice. He stated that there were two central forces that needed to be kept in balance: differentiation from family and fusion (togetherness) with one's family. Differentiation was defined as being intra- and interpersonal. 'Intrapersonal' meant that one could differentiate between thoughts and feelings; that is, it was possible to have strong emotions, and to remain rational and in control of personal cognitions. 'Interpersonal' meant that one was able not to overly react to others. The second force, fusion, taken at its extreme, meant that one was enmeshed in a dysfunctional family structure.

Bowen saw families as falling on a continuum between these two forces, with the healthier ones being closer to differentiation, where it was possible to think rationally yet continue to be emotionally connected to others. He also believed that present issues were rooted in multigenerational transmission processes (i.e. issues or processes that had been passed on from the family of origin to which the client was still emotionally fused); and that differentiation had to take place in the family of origin (West, 1994).

Another central premise of Bowen's was the principle of triangles. When two people (dyad) in a significant relationship are experiencing difficulties, they often distance themselves from each other to avoid confrontation. They accomplish this distancing by allowing a third person or thing to be triangled into their relationship. This can be seen during times of family loss when anxiety, stress, and grief are acute; instead of grieving together and supporting each other, the marital pair avoid issues of their loss and triangle a child into the relationship, focusing their attention on the child's issues at the expense of working on their own as a couple.

Lastly, Bowen's idea of the family projection process promoted insight into dysfunctional relationships between spouses who emotionally distance themselves from one another. A typical example is the situation in which the husband who has been emotionally cut off from his family of origin distances himself from his wife. She in turn overinvests in her children, with one child usually being the focus of her attention. However, Bowen drew attention to the term 'projection', and stated that it is different from loving concern. Projection promotes an enmeshed relationship, and often the child who has been the focus of attention will have the most difficulty with differentiation (Nichols & Schwartz, 1991).

Strategic theory

Strategic and systematic approaches share many similarities in their philosophy of family and their therapeutic approaches. Some of the commonalities include a 'systemic view' (i.e. the focus on the problem, rather than symptoms); planned strategic interventions to encourage change; and problem-solving, not family change, as the goal. Leading figures in this model were Jay Haley (1980), Cloe Madanes (1981), and members of the Mental Research Institute (MRI) in Palo Alto, California. These therapists viewed the family as a complex system, differentiated into hierarchies and arranged into subsystems, with the dysfunction in one subsystem being expressed in another. The term 'identified patient' referred to the family member who displayed the dysfunctional symptom to protect the family, with the family maintaining the symptom for purposes of homeostasis (West, 1994). Strategic therapists also borrowed from cybernetics, using concepts of rules to govern the system, with positive and negative feedback loops. Haley believed that rules were formed around the hierarchy in the family, and that this was often the core of family malfunctioning. Although the terms 'identified patient' and rules around a hierarchy are similar to Bowen's concept of a triangle, there is some difference in conceptualization between a hierarchy, determined by rules, and a triangle. An example would be parents whose marriage could not survive without having a child who is exhibiting behavioural problems. Their arguing initiates their son's acting-out behaviours, and attention then is directed to the child. The governing rules have the underlying message that the marriage would not be able to survive if they were free to discuss their problems without distraction from their son (Nichols & Schwartz, 1991).

Structural theory

Other researchers and therapists have favoured a structural approach to understanding and working with clients. A leading theorist in this area of structural family therapy was Salvador Minuchin. Minuchin (1974) focused on three constructs: structure, subsystems, and boundaries. Structure was defined as a pattern of organization in which family members interact in predictable sequences. These sequences are repeated and form enduring patterns of family behaviour. The patterns involve sets of covert rules that govern family transactions. Subsystems within a family are determined by generation, gender, or common interests. Minuchin theorized that families were differentiated into various subsystems to perform certain functions. He viewed every individual as a subsystem, with dyads and larger groups making up other subsystems. Family members play different roles in the various subsystems, and individual family members usually belong to more than one subsystem within a family structure. Lastly he proposed the concept of boundaries and stated that 'individuals, subsystems, and whole families are demarcated by *interpersonal boundaries*, invisible barriers that surround individuals and subsystems, regulating the amount of contact with others' (Nichols & Schwartz, 1991: 451). Boundaries are on a continuum between rigid (nothing is allowed to permeate) and diffuse (enmeshment, i.e. no sense of personal boundaries).

Constructivism

Lastly, principles from constructivism add insight and offer practical applications to family therapy. This theory has had a variety of interpretations, many of which have been controversial. One of the basic premises of this theory is that reality does not exist as a singular entity, but that there is more than one reality. This concept is a core principle of postmodern thinking. Within family therapy this philosophy has been used to facilitate a different way of assessing and conceptualizing family issues. Counsellors have become more aware of the fact that they were viewing right and wrong and good and bad based on their own values. Previously, professionals in the helping professions imposed their meanings of reality upon clients, especially upon families. Constructivism asks these professionals 'not to consider what they are seeing in families as existing in the family but, instead, understand what they are seeing is the product of their particular set of assumptions about people, families, and problems, and their interactions with the family' (Nichols & Schwartz, 1991: 142).

This theory has particular relevance for bereavement counselling. It has been our experience that the advice offered to those in grief, in large part, is based on personal experiences and belief systems. Such a frame of reference more often impedes than promotes healthy resolution. As proposed in the underlying tenets of this approach, counsellors should be collaborators in a process, and not the experts. Only the individual client or family knows the depth and meaning of their grief experience. We cannot and must not put all grievers into presupposed categories, treating them all the same, based on a presumed category of their loss. A bereaved mother will not have the same issues or experience as another bereaved mother, even if they have lost a child the same age in the same circumstances.

The following case highlights some of the theories and principles discussed regarding concepts of family, tasks of family development, and concepts of family therapy.

The Smith family: death of the oldest daughter

Presenting problem

The Smith family sought counselling because the behaviour of the 12-year-old boy was out of control, and the mother (who initiated counselling) stated that she could not tolerate his behaviour any more. The family consisted of Mary (mother, aged 39); Joe (father, aged 39); Jamie (daughter, aged 20, deceased); Carol (daughter, aged 13); Harry (son, aged 12); Mark (son, aged 10); Jill and Jim (twins, aged 3). The 12-year-old son had received detentions in school for his misbehaviour, was failing two subjects, was refusing to obey his mother, and in general kept the household in uproar. He was influencing his 10-year-old brother to the point that his sibling had begun to join him in some of his antics. The father could control them; however, he was gone (working) from early morning to 7 or 8 p.m. each day. The mother demanded obedience from her children and displayed little tolerance of any transgressions. She was a compulsive house-cleaner and had specific expectations regarding chores to be completed on a daily basis by the children. She also feared for their safety (even before the death of her daughter). This fear had resulted in strict boundary rules. The children never rode a school bus and during their free time they could not travel beyond their street. The 12-year-old had been challenging many of these rules.

Family life-cycle and external sources of stress

Following Duvall and Miller (1985) this family was simultaneously working at three distinct stages (see Table 4.1, p. 66). First, they had reached Stage 5 (oldest child between 13 and 20). The oldest daughter had been a college student living on campus about 12 miles from home. She had been striving for her freedom, although her mother had attempted to thwart her efforts towards differentiation. In addition to the mother's unwillingness to let go, having five younger children made it impossible for the parents even to consider establishing postparental interests, a developmental task of this stage. Another stage influencing this family's life-cycle was Stage 4 (ages 6–13). Tasks during this part of the cycle include fitting into the community of school-age families and encouraging children's educational achievement. Due to the external stressor of the accidental death of their eldest daughter a year ago, this developmental task was not being addressed on an ongoing basis. It was addressed from crisis to crisis. That is, failing grades and misbehaviour were the only motivators for these parents to be involved with three of their children. Lastly, this family was involved in the tasks of Stage 3 (2½–6). This period emphasizes the need to attend to critical issues of young children's development; yet it also has the potential to deplete the energy of the parents and invade their sense of privacy. Coupled with the stress of grief, there was little energy or interest in the needs of the twins. The 13-year-old daughter was expected to fulfil this task. The multiple levels of the family life-cycle, the varied developmental tasks imposed by each level, and the external stressor of the sudden, unexpected death of the first-born were the factors underlying assessment and therapeutic intervention with this family.

Family subsystems

Families are differentiated into *subsystems* of members who join together to perform various functions. Viewing the family in this structural way recognizes that these subsystems have boundaries separating them. In the family described above, the subsystems were many and varied, with the majority lacking clear boundaries, especially generational ones. A powerful subsystem had been the mother and the deceased daughter. The mother described her as her best friend. She had been born when she (the mother) was 18, and according to her perspective, 'they had grown up together'. Jamie was the parental child and had kept the marriage together. As her siblings were born, she had assumed parental duties. The marital dyad, as a subsystem, was dysfunctional from the first year of marriage. Joe was not approved by his wife's family, and her family of origin continued to exert a powerful influence on their lives. During the first year of her marriage Mary spent a great deal of her time caring for her mother (mother–daughter subsystem) after her brother, James, died in an accident. Her mother became bedridden, stricken with grief after the death of her son. Mary's daughter (Jamie), who was born during this period, was named after the deceased brother at the request of her parents. Her father, a successful businessman, controlled his children and their spouses by employing them in his company. At the time of counselling, Joe had been working for his father-in-law for 21 years. He had never been fully accepted, but had few skills to work elsewhere.

Within the nuclear family there were several other subsystems. Joe appeared to be a peripheral member in most of these. It was unclear how he viewed himself in the father–daughter (deceased) subsystem. Observing his grief, it did not appear to be a 'parental' grieving response. It had characteristics that one might observe after the loss of a spouse. Perhaps his daughter represented what he wanted in a wife. After the death of Jamie, Mary continued a subsystem with her through the use of mourning rituals and graveside visits. She did not turn to her husband in grief (nor he to her); rather, she sought to create a new subsystem with Carol, as she pushed the role of parental child on to her.

The children had their own groupings. As mentioned, Carol (13) had been manoeuvred into a subsystem with the three-year-old twins, and the 10- and 12-year-old boys were aligning to form a disruptive subsystem. They had clearly defined boundaries in their system, which included only the two of them, with the distinct purpose of defying the parental authority of their mother. They had a considerable amount of power, which they exercised on a daily basis. At the time that counselling was sought, Harry (12) was the identified patient.

In the extended family, there were several systems that were operating. In addition to the parents from the mother's family of origin, there were subsystems (mother's side) that involved five married siblings, their spouses, and their children. Joe had come from a dysfunctional family and had totally severed ties with them over 20 years ago.

Repetitive behavioural sequences in family boundaries and hierarchy

Behavioural sequences were apparent within the nuclear family and Mary's family of origin. Differentiation had not occurred and the boundaries were poorly differentiated between the nuclear family and the extended family. Mary had never created her own identity, separating herself mentally and emotionally from her parents or siblings. The larger extended family was enmeshed, with Mary's father at the helm, controlling jobs and income (repetitive behavioural sequence). His financial control ensured that they would all continue to dance together to his tune.

Growing up, Mary had been the 'identified patient' in her family. She had been labelled frail and weak, and had been hospitalized at the age of 12 with a 'nervous breakdown'. She had been unable to handle the stress of school. Behavioural sequences, reflecting emotional instability as a reaction to conflict or stress, recurred throughout her adult life. Three times when she could not address her husband's threats of leaving, she attempted suicide. Suicide was also attempted the night the daughter died and during the course of family counselling. The discord in the marital and parental hierarchy had never been directly addressed. Moreover, the couple did not complete their divorce because of the births of their children. The births were another repeated sequence that provided sufficient distraction to take attention away from the marital conflicts.

Other repetitive sequences that reflected discord in both hierarchy and boundaries were the continued efforts to create a parental child. Jamie was the first and Carol was becoming the second, enabling a triangular relationship to continue. Another repetitive behaviour was to focus on the misbehaviours of the children, with Harry being the current identified patient. Mary continued to feel overwhelmed and out of control, but changed none of her own behaviours. She napped during the day, abdicated her responsibilities for the twins, shouted at the boys, and went out three nights a week with girlfriends to get away from the children. Harry had perfected a script for his misbehaviour and Mary was pulled into it regularly. Joe remained peripheral, but was called in at the eleventh hour to be the disciplinarian. The behaviours brought him back into the system, but kept the focus off the marital dyad. There were several other behavioural sequences that were unproductive in terms of family functioning; however, the ones mentioned serve to highlight the issues underlying this family's structure. It is important to note that continued enmeshment with the family of origin was a core feature of the present family system.

The family problem/symptom: how it maintains the system

System maintenance for this family included issues and relationships that were current in the nuclear family, but were also part of a multigenerational transmission process. Although the mother was also an identified patient, she was not getting the focus as the patient from her nuclear family, but continued to get it from her family of origin. The present symptoms of misbehaviour from Harry kept the focus off the marital conflicts, thus keeping the marriage together.

Joe had come into this marriage from a dysfunctional background. Bowen (1978) discusses the family projection process. In keeping with Bowen's description, this man had severed all ties with his family of origin and was only able to relate to his wife in a cool and distant manner. As a result she focused intensely on her first-born, Jamie. However, this was not loving concern. As projection, it was an anxious, enmeshed concern. And with the subsequent children she had been emotionally distant.

Grief as a symptom and how it could maintain the family system was not considered during the initial counselling sessions with this family. It had been less than a year since the death had occurred; and adhering to the concepts of parental grief (Rando, 1993), it was important to keep in mind that there are issues in this type of loss/grief that make it complicated. Thus, it can be expected that grief reactions on the part of parents that may appear bizarre and pathological are often within the norms of parental grief. However, considering the pre-morbid characteristics of this family, it is conceivable that grief could maintain this system. The marital dyad would be able to stay together, but focus on the loss and grief issues. This family could remain resistant to any type of change, and could use any available issues/symptoms to self-regulate and maintain homeostasis.

With the passage of another year, and after initial family sessions and individual sessions for the children and Mary, it became apparent that this family would remain together, using grief to maintain the system.

Interventions

Interventions were based on the above assessments. Individual and family issues were kept in mind and addressed as they emerged in the sessions. Mary's primary issues were her unrelenting acute grief, her dissatisfaction with the lack of support that she perceived from her husband, and her inability to cope with and control her children, especially Harry. The family as a unit focused more on the overall disorganization and unhappiness of everyday living, the acting-out behaviours of Harry, normal pre-teen issues of Carol and Mark, and the trials of coping with three-year-old twins. The family as a unit addressed their grief indirectly. There was no visible demonstration of a family grieving together, nor was there any evidence that the members shared any of the same grief issues. As asserted by Raphael:

> Bereavement will affect the family system in many ways. The death of a member means the system is irrevocably changed. Interlocking roles, relationships, interactions, communications, and psychopathology and needs can no longer be fulfilled in the same way as before the death. The family unit as it was before dies, and a new family system must be constituted. The death will be a crisis for the family unit as well as for each individual member and each component subsystem. The family view of itself, the family myth, may be impossible to maintain, and all that it avoided may have to be confronted. The threat to the integrity of the family unit may come not only through the change that loss of a family member brings, but also because that member may have occupied a key role in maintaining the system, or perhaps in regulating it in crisis. (1983: 54)

Another factor to be mindful of is the fact that members of a family are usually not in the same stage of their grief experience at the same time, even though their grief is emerging from the same event, thus making it difficult to muster emotional resources for each other on a consistent basis. And lastly, each person in a family has had a unique relationship with the deceased, thus necessitating different issues to grieve and resolve. Family discord can arise and cause additional grief if family members fail to see each other as individuals, with idiosyncratic ways of grieving, coping, and resolving their pain.

As an individual in counselling prior to family counselling, Mary was allowed much time to share her pain and to create appropriate rituals to work through her grief. Memorialization was a major focus of the intervention strategies. This will be discussed at greater length in Chapter 5. Another major focus was to co-design a treatment plan that would improve her daily functioning, especially as it related to the care and well-being of her other children.

In sessions that involved the entire family, it was important to have another counsellor involved who did not know Mary and could assure the family that he was neutral and there to listen to their concerns. Mary had established a relationship with her counsellor for over six months, so the other family members were initially concerned that the counsellor would support only Mary's views. Moreover, a male counsellor provided a role model for the husband and two sons. The three-year-old twins were not present during the sessions. The issues that were most burdensome to the family were initially addressed, with the intention to help the family achieve better levels of daily functioning before addressing the impact that Jamie's death had upon the family unit. It was quickly assessed that the husband/father was not emotionally close to the family and lacked involvement in virtually every dimension. Thus an early attempt in the sessions was to bring him into the family and validate his role.

C(M): Joe, thanks for taking time out of your work schedule to meet with the family for these sessions. It is important that you can be here also to help your family find ways to work together. When there's a death in the family, no one is sure what to do any more.

Joe: I don't know if we ever worked together, even before Jamie's death. As long as I bring home the week's income that's all they care about.

Mary: That's not true. I tried to show you that I care. But you're the one who shows that you don't care. I went and planned a birthday party for you, and you didn't even want to go. Then when you did go, you drank all night.

Joe: That's not what I am talking about. I'm talking about how you ignore the kids or yell at them. When I come home, you walk out. Three nights a week you go out to relax and get away from the kids. But I don't see you putting yourself out for them when you are home.

Harry: Mum, Dad's right; you don't care about anyone any more. You are always sleeping; and when you aren't you make us work: 'Take out the garbage, watch the twins, do this, do that . . .'

Mary: Well, you don't do anything I tell you to do, so why should I get up? I can't control you, and your father is never home to help out.

C(M): Joe, it sounds like Mary really depends on you to help with the children also.

Joe: No, she just gets them mad by her constant nagging and screaming, then they torment her by mouthing off to her.

*C(M) = counsellor/male
*C(F) = counsellor/female

Then she expects me to come home and straighten up the mess. To tell you the truth, I work as late as I can to avoid the fights.

*C(F): Has it always been like this for this family? What I mean is, was it different (more cooperation) before Jamie died?

Joe: The only difference was that Jamie took over. She took care of the twins, and kept her brothers in line. Mary never was able to cope with the kids. She depended upon Jamie, and got mad at her when she wanted to go out with her friends.

This exchange allows the counsellors to understand some of the hierarchy and structure of the family. Jamie's role had been important for the functioning of the family. The male counsellor, early in the session, attempted to bring the husband/father into the family and validate his status. Joe's response indicated that he had a negative view of himself and his role in the family. The female counsellor attempted to assess if there was a difference in how the family interacted since the death of Jamie, and the response indicated that Mary's role may not have changed that much. Early in the session it became apparent that Jamie was the parental child and that a significant role in the family had been lost with her death. Attempts were made throughout the session to connect the loss of roles and the change in the family structure since Jamie's death to current turmoil and dysfunction. At the end of this session, the family agreed to have a family meeting on Sundays after church to discuss chores, privileges, concerns, gripes, and so forth. Joe was instructed to conduct these meetings. At this point, he seemed committed to this initial plan and asserted that something had to change. Joe also agreed to take responsibility for disciplining Harry and Mark.

Sessions continued with this family for several months. Joe followed through with his commitment to carry out discipline and handle problems with Harry and Mark; however, the family meetings on Sundays never materialized. Moreover, he began to miss counselling sessions, which greatly changed the focus of the interventions and the family dynamics during the sessions. Without the physical presence and backing of their father, the boys did not express their opinion towards their mother as much. They became more passive, and sessions focused more on conflicts between Carol and Mary, and Carol's resistance to assuming the role of her deceased sister.

Carol: I don't know why I can't go out for athletics training. I can't do anything any more with your expectations of me.

Mary: Well, Jamie helped me raise the twins. Here's a picture of her with the twins on her lap [*She hands a picture to the counsellor*.] Isn't she beautiful? Doesn't she look like a natural mother? She always wanted to be a mother. Now she never will be. [*Sobs*].

Carol: I can't be Jamie. I don't want to be. I don't even miss her. She was all yours. We had nothing in common with each other; she was seven years older than me.

Mary: I don't want you to be her. I just don't want to have to be bothered with any of you now. I am too tired.

Carol: [*jumps topics*] Why can't I have her bedroom? You have the twins in my room with me, and you go to sleep on Jamie's bed after Dad goes to sleep.

Mary: No one is going to use that room yet. I'm not ready to change it around. It has only been nine months, and that's where I go and feel close to her.

C(F): Carol, it sounds like you were asking your mum a few things. I heard her answer some of your concerns; but the first question you asked was about going out training, and that was never addressed after you brought it up. Can we go back to that?

Mary: Well, I think that Carol should realize that we are all going through a bad time right now, and that she cannot expect me to manage one more thing, like picking her up every day from practice, and bringing her to games.

Carol: I can get friends' parents to bring me home. I have already asked them.

Mary: You had no right to do that. [*Turns to talk to female counsellor*.] She has no idea what I am going through. None of my kids do. They want everything they want, and they don't care about me, or even miss Jamie.

C(F): Why don't you turn around and look at Carol and tell her what you are telling me, Mary, so she can see how you are feeling.

The relationship that Mary had with her deceased daughter was exclusive, and none of the children could begin to understand her grief. Carol had experienced Mary's grief, but had resented it. In session, the counsellor first brought attention back to Carol's opening question to clarify the request before addressing the grief issues. Mary continued to distort this request, seeing it as an additional burden to her grief. In order to break the pattern of miscommunication and distorted communications of grief, the counsellor asked Mary to turn and face her daughter and tell her directly what she had just told the counsellor. This was an attempt to facilitate a direct and honest expression of grief by Mary to her daughter. Up to this point, it was not clear what the issues of grief were for any family member other than Mary. Using the opportunity to get the mother to face the daughter and express herself was an opening to go back and ask questions about the bedroom and the relationship that the siblings had with Jamie. As assessed, the relationship with Carol was distant; however, the relationship with Harry, Mark and the twins was that of a mother figure. Part of the turmoil, disorganization, and acting-out was because they had lost the direction from the real mother figure, Jamie.

Ongoing sessions moved to individual ones, as Joe refused to return, and it became apparent that Harry and Mark needed attention from the male counsellor on an individual basis to gain understanding of the meaning and nature of the relationship that they had with their older sister. Carol went into individual counselling with a third (female) counsellor, who worked well with adolescents. In her sessions, she clarified her relationship with her sister, her grief, and her emerging developmental issues of adolescence. Her counsellor encouraged Mary to acknowledge and allow the normal adolescent needs of Carol. Mary continued in individual counselling for another year and participated in a support group that had three other bereaved mothers.

Grief issues for individual family members

Family members do not grieve the same, and often do not have the same issues. Each person in a family had his or her unique relationship with a deceased member, thus necessitating an idiosyncratic grief experience. The following offers some guidelines for pertinent issues of various family members, following a death in the family.

Death of a spouse

The death of a spouse includes the loss of many roles. The spouse was not only a husband or a wife, in the broadest sense; he or she was friend, confidant, lover, provider, supporter, and sometimes 'the better half'. Often a spouse is the primary person who confirms one's sense of identity and self-worth. Adjusting an identity from a 'we' to an 'I' is one of the poignant issues to contend with. Very often, one's social world also ends with the death of a spouse. The loneliness experienced will be physical, sexual, social, and emotional. This type of death affects the family in various ways, with different issues. One of the primary factors for consideration is the age of the children and all the related issues and concerns associated with this.

Death of a parent

As an adult, when one's parent dies, the experience is often a lonely and unrecognized loss. Many do not live where their parents live; thus most of the friends who would attend the funeral or be available for support have little to offer because of their lack of association with the deceased parent. Moreover, this death is often not socially sanctioned, because we are told that we should expect our parents to die before us. Parents have a unique role in our lives. They are the first relationship and are our ties back to our past and our childhood. As long as parents are alive, it is possible to deny one's own mortality, as they are a buffer between oneself and death. When it is the death of a second parent, the individual experiences what it is like to be an orphan.

Various other issues emerge depending upon one's age at the time of a parent's death. An example is a 20-year-old male whose father died of a heart attack at the age of 56. The grief reactions and fears of one's own mortality may become more acute when that son approaches his 56th birthday (anniversary reaction). When a parent dies during one's childhood or adolescence, one should keep in mind for these age groups that the loss of a parent must be understood according to the developmental level of the child or adolescent, and that normal developmental tasks must be addressed. Moreover, this age group relies upon denial, repression, and suppression. Grief may not be fully addressed or resolved until early adulthood. Children and adolescents must grieve fully; however, they must be allowed to do so on their timetables, and with ongoing, available support systems. With each stage of development, new questions and new issues will emerge that need to be re-examined and answered in light of more cognitive and emotional growth.

Death of a sibling

At any age, the death of a sibling has its own unique issues. A sibling shares similar, genetic characteristics with you. This is an individual (in addition to one's parents) in whom one can often see a reflection of oneself. This is a person with whom one has shared a unique co-history, often marked by ambivalence and more difficult issues to grieve.

When a sibling dies the surviving sibling(s) experience a variety of thoughts and feelings. Often the survivor feels that the 'favourite' child has died, and that it is important to take on characteristics or behaviours of the deceased to lessen the grief of the parents. Role reversals (children assuming parental roles) also occur in attempts to alleviate parental pain. Guilt is a frequent emotion, as many siblings have harboured ill will towards each other over the years; and the reality of the death is difficult to adjust to. Many siblings have lost a close and trusted companion, and the grief will emerge during many milestones of their childhood and adult life. Davies (1990), in a seven-year longitudinal study of siblings who had died from cancer, found that siblings frequently thought of the deceased and grieved. Life had moved on; but thoughts and feelings were close at hand.

For many adults whose siblings die, the current support systems may be unaware of the special bond that may have continued for years. In mobile societies people may not live where they were born, so present friends and potential support systems may not know what to say or do. This often increases a sense of aloneness in one's grief, as it is difficult to feel connected to those around who were not part of this relationship.

Death of a child
No other loss has as many issues, and there is no other role that is governed by more rules or social sanctions. It is referred to as the one area in family life where society will step in and take over if the responsible adults do not perform according to certain dictates. Thus, when a child dies, the parents experience incredible guilt for a role in which they have not succeeded. There are differences in the ways males and females grieve; and when this is not understood, it may cause discord in the marital dyad. There may be problems parenting other children, and if one of the spouses closely resembles the deceased child this causes additional pain. This type of grief cannot be compared to any other type of loss, and counsellors should avoid trying to fit it into a current model for grief resolution.

A common question following the death of a child is the concern over potential, future divorce. Many believe that statistics are high for divorce following the death of a child, yet others do not see the correlation between death and divorce. Rando (1993) believes that statistics have inaccurately represented the reasons for a divorce following the death of a child. Her view is that the divorces that do occur represent marriages that had previously been troubled; and following the death of a child, one of the partners will make the decision that he or she is not going to put up with any extra grief. That is, they express the fact that they had endured a difficult marriage before the death, but now they only have the energy to deal with the death that is at hand. From a systems viewpoint, the triangular third party that allowed the marriage to continue is no longer available.

Family losses other than death
Death is not the only loss that most families have to cope with during their life-cycle. Moreover, death is often not the most difficult

or deleterious loss. Illness, desertion, divorce, abuse, job loss, and disasters, such as fires and floods, are a few that can be mentioned. Although general concepts and theories of loss may be used, along with tools such as the 'Perspectives', 'Experiences of grief', the 'History of loss', and 'Psychological needs assessment', these losses will have specific issues to address, cope with, and resolve. It is beyond the scope of this book to thoroughly discuss every type of loss; a case example illustrating the effects of mental illness, alcoholism, and divorce will be presented to highlight some of the different effects and demands that other losses have on a family.

Dave: a young adult with an uncertain future

Dave, a 27-year-old, initiated counselling on his own after his younger half-brother, aged 17, was arrested for theft. This event seemed to trigger past, unresolved issues in his life and to emphasize the bleakness of his present life and uncertain future. 'A history of loss' (Table 4.2) was used after the first session, when it became apparent that Dave had multiple losses in his life that had never been resolved. The first session also made the counsellor aware of the fact that his issues were rooted in his family of origin and two blended family systems. When he sought counselling, he was living 50 miles away from his family, but he had never differentiated himself from them, especially from his father. His father had remarried a few years earlier, and was living with his third wife, her children, and a son (a half-brother of Dave) from the second marriage. Dave's biological mother was deceased; and his stepmother, an alcoholic, was living alone, having recently lost custody of her two biological sons. His father had divorced his stepmother during Dave's sophomore year in high school.

For five years before the divorce, Dave experienced much turmoil and disintegration of the family unit as his stepmother unsuccessfully attempted to deal with alcoholism. The onset of her alcoholism seemed sudden, with no warning that she had been experiencing any emotional difficulties. He could remember many wonderful years with his stepmother. His father had remarried and seemed very happy. His two half-brothers had been born, and the family was close-knit and involved in each other's lives in a meaningful way. Suddenly it seemed as if that was over. He never even knew she drank; and then abruptly it was destroying six people's lives. He spent his last three years in high school torn between two homes.

After high school, all he could think of was getting as far away as possible. He almost failed his senior year; however, he had signed up for military service, and he was able to persuade the school to

Table 4.2 *History of loss – case of 'Dave'*

Loss	Age	Experiences (feelings/behaviours)	Unanswered questions	What changed (money, residence, etc.)
Death of mother	5	Sadness, confusion	How did she die?	Moved; dad remarried
Alcoholism (Stepmother)	15	Hospitalizations, family fights, scared, lonely	Why? What made this happen?	Divorce
Discharge from military (dishonourable)	22	Shame, fear, confusion, ran, drifted alone	Why didn't I get help? Why did I try to kill myself?	No roots, no purpose in life
Younger brother arrested	27	Horror, shame	What has happened to our family?	Sought counselling for the first time

graduate him. He spent four years in the military, and was asked to leave after several misdemeanours and an unsuccessful suicide attempt. There was no counselling for him after this; the military discharged him as quickly as possible. For the next five years he drifted, taking odd jobs for minimum pay, never having a permanent place of residence. Shortly after his half-brother's arrest, he suddenly realized that his life was slipping away from him and he needed help.

During the second session, the counsellor suggested that they review together the many losses that he had experienced in order to understand more clearly his present situation. The 'history of loss' revealed multiple losses and changes from the age of four onwards, that had never been explained, understood, or experienced in a healthy manner. Resolution of all these past losses had never been possible, because Dave had been protected from the truth about them.

As the 'history of loss' was being constructed, both Dave and the counsellor began to get a visual representation of multiple disruptions and abrupt changes throughout his life that had resulted in many unanswered questions. Often a place to start with a client who presents multiple losses is to investigate whether or not there have been issues left unresolved. Not understanding why a loss has happened because the correct information has never been given is often the case, and this is where the intervention can begin. Another technique is to ask the client which loss they would like to address first. Many choose to start with the least threatening loss, in order to become comfortable with the procedure and experience of making oneself vulnerable for the pain that will emerge from repressed losses. Dave chose to start at the beginning with the death of his biological mother.

> *D*: I never fully understood why my mother died. I was only four, so I was too young (they said) to go to the funeral.
>
> *C*: If I understand you correctly, you still do not understand the cause of your mother's death.
>
> *D*: I asked a lot of questions, but I don't even remember what I was told. I was only four at the time; and even years later I'd still ask, but was told that it happened a long time ago, and that it was over. But I don't think it's ever been over for me.
>
> *C*: You are right. It is important to have the correct information about what happened. Without this, you have a difficult time letting go and healing. The mind searches for reasons and a loss has to be understood, as much as it possibly can be.
>
> *D*: I often think that my problems and my dad's have something to do with my mother's death. One week after the funeral we

moved here. My sister was a year older than I was and she didn't know much either. Dad got a good job here and he said we were all going to start a new life together. We had no family here, so we had lots of different babysitters while he was at work. Then he met Sue who lived in the apartment next to us. She began to watch us after school, and we all liked her. My dad ended up marrying her two years after we moved here. Everything seemed to be like he said it was going to be: we were happy and starting a new life. To tell you the truth, I never thought a lot about my mum after that until this thing with Sue started.

C: Do you mean her problem with alcohol?

D: Yes. We didn't even know why she was in the hospital for a month. I was 11 then; but it still seemed like my dad never told us kids anything. He couldn't say we were too young any more. I just figured that was the way he was. But I was scared because I wondered if Sue would die too. When she came home from the hospital, she told us all about it. She said she didn't feel ashamed because alcoholism was a disease and she needed all of us to help her fight it.

C: Was the family able to work together with this problem?

D: For a while. I think things went OK for about six months. Then Dad started being mean to her and telling her she couldn't do anything right. After he started that, then Sue would start drinking again. This went on, and she was in and out of treatment centres until they divorced when I was 15. Dad married his secretary two weeks after the divorce. I think there had been a relationship between them for a long time. At times I think he was mean to Mum to get rid of her. But then, looking back, I don't think Dad was ever really happy; and I don't think he is now.

C: That brings us back to your mum's death, and your feeling that there's a lot of unhappiness that's somehow connected to it.

D: Yes, I don't think it has anything to do with Sue's problem, but it seems to have a lot to do with Dad's ways.

C: Is there anyone you could get some information from?

D: Maybe my mother's sister. We don't see her often, but she and my mum were always close.

Dave subsequently learned from his aunt that his mother had committed suicide; and not surprisingly, many had blamed his dad. His mother was an artist, very quiet and introverted; however, her sister felt that his father had spent more time trying to get ahead in his business than attending to his wife and two young children. There had not been a suicide note to explain her pain and desperation; so for everyone, there remained unanswered questions and issues of blame. Dave could live with not having full understanding of the reasons for the suicide; however, he had not been able to live with not knowing how she died. Once he learned about the suicide, he was then able to address the other issues of loss. In addition to insight, Dave also had to learn (and accept) appropriate expression of feelings. Family rules had never allowed emotions to be validated or expressed; moreover, communication between family members was never the norm. He came to view his stepmother as a vulnerable human being, whose weaknesses had emerged in a dysfunctional family system.

Writing letters to those with whom he had unfinished business was a primary intervention. He initially chose to write letters to his deceased mother (following the format used in Chapter 5), his father, and his stepmother. The instructions were to write the letters without prior thought in order to allow free expression of genuine emotions; then bring them to sessions and read them to the counsellor. After sharing them in sessions, the counsellor brought past experiences with significant people in his life into a here-and-now focus. This was accomplished by reflecting to Dave the feelings that she was experiencing from him as she listened:

C: I can hear the anger in your voice and your hands are shaking as you are telling your dad in the letter that you feel that he is worthless as a human being and worse than a murderer.

D: Yes. I never felt this way about him before. I never had any feelings because he was always such a mystery. When you can't figure someone out and they aren't around you that much, it's hard to know what you are feeling. But writing these letters helped because I can look at what I wrote and see myself for the first time.

After sharing the letters over a number of sessions and processing them together, Dave decided how to dispose of them. Because his mother's letter was poignant and elicited much pain, he felt that it belonged with her in the graveyard, beneath the ground near the top of her tombstone. The second letter (for his stepmother) he gave directly to her. This symbolically shared his understanding of her condition and expressed his love for her. His father's letter expressed bitterness and anger that he had not been in touch with. This letter he chose to burn. Sessions with Dave continued for over a year, focusing on issues of loss, grief, and rebuilding.

Every individual in counselling represents, and has been influenced by, at least one family. Losses within a family unit (past or present family systems) mean that a family, as it had once existed and had been known, is now dead. Although counsellors mostly see individuals in counselling, it is important to consider the concepts and examples presented in this chapter for a more in-depth assessment and understanding of underlying issues as they pertain to individuals as members of some type of family.

5

Group Counselling

Group counselling offers an excellent choice for therapeutic intervention. It is not the intention to recommend groups over individual counselling; the intention is to highlight some of the contributions of group counselling in general, to discuss specific features of grief groups, and to outline various components of the sessions of structured groups that can facilitate the process of grief counselling.

Therapeutic factors in groups

A group is a representation of the family and community to which individuals belong. Issues that emerge in a group often have origins in past and present family and community relationships. Often the dynamics of interpersonal relationships are not on a conscious level of awareness. For many, the group experience will offer the initial experience of personal insight into their relationships with others. Within the format of the group, a process occurs that is not possible in individual counselling. There are more people to relate to and common issues of the human condition emerge that facilitate exploration of personal issues. Yalom (1985) proposed 11 primary factors that he viewed as being the basis of the therapeutic experience of group work: instillation of hope, universality, imparting of information, altruism, the corrective recapitulation of a family group, development of socializing techniques, imitative behaviour, interpersonal learning, group cohesiveness, catharsis, and existential factors (1985: 3–4).

Individuals attending a grief group have the opportunity to experience many of the above-mentioned influences. Instillation of hope occurs as members observe positive changes in each other and anticipate forward movement in their own process of bereavement. As they take risks to fully experience the pain of grief, they come to understand that the pain will not further destroy them; instead the pain becomes a healing element. The universality of some of the common aspects of grief promotes a bonding and a sense that one is not alone in grief. However, although grief is the common denominator, initially individual differences will need attention. Members may not be experiencing the same type of death nor the same issues. Even within a family, no two members will have the same grief experience. The relationship each person has had with the deceased has been different, and the various perspectives discussed in Chapters 1, 2, and 3 will influence each person's grief process in a different manner. In the early, acute period of grief an individual will not feel connected to others. They believe that their grief is more painful than anyone else's, and they do not want theirs to be compared to another's grief experience. From a philosophical perspective, one must face this aloneness, meaninglessness, and despair in isolation before one can connect with others in the universal aspects of grief. There seems to be a sense of readiness to connect with others and be part of a group six to eight weeks following a death. Before this time there are pervasive feelings of unreality, numbness, and a general desire to turn inward in one's grief. To experience a universality that promotes cohesion and a sense of belonging takes time and willingness on the part of members to risk joining with others. Many express reluctance at self-disclosure because they believe that others will not view their issues as valid or important. Many individuals remain lonely in their grief because they believe their needs to be petty or selfish.

Early on, members need to know if their individual needs will be met in a group where they view themselves as being different from others, even though they are there for similar reasons. From the first session the group is structured to foster an atmosphere and environment that assures members that their needs will be met. The promotion of universality and cohesiveness in the sessions builds hope. Those in grief together begin to rely on each other; they can begin to hope for diminished pain and new futures. They begin to learn from each other and realize that mourning will not be for ever.

Members know from the first session who will be in the group. This facilitates the process of building trust and cohesiveness. They start to share with each other what they have experienced, how they have felt, and how they have coped. This sharing of information and resources with each other is a source of group strength. As this occurs, members begin to support each other and experience further healing from their efforts of altruism. They begin to understand that their grief is lessened by helping others in similar circumstances.

As mentioned above, members want to know if their needs will be met in this group. All have come from some type of family group, with positive and negative experiences. Many have been told by family members that they should 'get on' with their lives, or that their grief is a sign of weakness. The support group has the potential to be a corrective recapitulation of a family. Members will find someone in the group who reminds them of a family member. Thus an event that occurred many years ago within someone's family can still be experienced, cognitively and emotionally, in present time. Through the power of the experience of the group, members can address past experiences, rethink and cognitively correct them, and understand their influence on the present experiences. Connections will be made, and members may see that they are reacting to a present situation that has components which represent something in the past. Opportunities are present to practise new behaviours that can be used in real-life settings. Generally speaking, a group has the potential to become a therapeutic community, offering opportunities for support, self-exploration, insight, behaviour change, and the development of new socializing techniques. Bereaved members often express the fact that they no longer hear from old friends, or that they feel that people are avoiding them because of their grief. Within a group setting, members accept and support each other in their grief, and move together to develop new skills for socialization. One support group had four widowers, who had been totally dependent upon their wives to provide their social life. After the third session, one of the men suggested that they all meet for dinner each week before the group. He said that he had never done anything like this before, but if women could have their hen parties, men could have their rooster parties.

Groups set the stage for imitative behaviour. Members will observe how others try to cope with their grief and imitate each other's efforts. This is especially true when someone comes in and reports that the pain of grief did not defeat him/her this week, and that a way had been found to cope with it. In the course of a several-session group most members will adopt aspects of each other's ways of behaving. This illustrates interpersonal learning; that is, the group learns from each other, not just from the counsellor. Those in pain are often the best teachers for each other, as they have acutely known the experience of grief. Basic information for surviving and coping is shared on a weekly basis. This type of interpersonal learning cannot take place in individual counselling.

Group cohesiveness is one of the most therapeutic factors in a bereavement support group. Members, whose worlds have been made less rich after the death of a loved one, need cohesion or a sense of belonging. They all enter a group feeling shattered and bereft. The trappings of pretence and the wearing of masks is usually not part of a group experiencing deep grief. The outer layers of human defences are cut through more quickly and a sense of cohesiveness and trust are more readily built. Activities, such as sharing pictures and stories about the deceased person, promote the goals of cohesiveness. Catharsis in a group that fosters a healthy expression of emotions is an integral factor, and one that needs little facilitation. Counsellors may have to state up front that sharing tears together is encouraged, and that it is a way to build inter- and intrapersonal strength.

Lastly, consideration is given to Yalom's existential factors brought to the surface by grief. As discussed in Chapter 1, existential anxieties are part of the philosophical perspective in the loss experience. Sharing common feelings of a deep sense of aloneness and questioning the meaning of life leads to the development of cohesiveness, and directs the process towards integration of the experience of loss and eventual rebuilding and resolution.

To illustrate the emotional connection among group members, the following letter reveals the personal experience of one member:

My Dear Friends,

Tonight is our last session together as a group but I hope it's not our last time together as friends. When I first came here, and for about the first four weeks, I thought I couldn't possibly continue the grief sessions, but for some unknown reason to me, I continued to come back, and now I am very sorry to see it end.

You have all reached out to me and touched my life, and through our mutual grief, we have come to know one another, and to care for one another. You have tried to help me understand the whys and have tried to show me reasons why I must go on and somehow, someday, perhaps be able to build a new and meaningful life for myself.

I will never forget your kindness and your love, our coffee breaks after the meetings, and your allowing me to share my dear and precious son with all of you. I know that if I never see some of you again on this earth, there will come a time when we shall be together with our loved ones and with each other on the other side of the mountain. (43 year old bereaved mother)

The following is an illustration of a semi-structured adult support group which capitalizes on Yalom's (1985) therapeutic factors.

Adult ten-week support group*

The adult 10-week group is semi-structured. Each session has a theme related to grief, the process, and potential resolution; individual needs

* Although this group is for death-related loss, it can be redesigned to address any loss. For example, this format has also been used for divorce and work-related losses. The sessions can use the same themes, but address the specific issues of the loss involved.

are addressed as they emerge, and the facilitator must be flexible enough and trust the group process to put the agenda aside as needed. The group has closed membership (8 to 12), with specific goals and objectives for each session. Although a grief group is mainly supportive, it also has the goal of education, or imparting information as described by Yalom. The educational portion of the group sessions is an essential component of intervention as there is often a lack of accurate information about the grief process. Information shared not only validates and normalizes the grief experience; it also educates members in healthy ways of expression and resolution.

Selection and screening
This group is intended for those individuals who are experiencing grief following the death of a significant person in their lives. The group is not intended for those who have additional and perhaps more intense issues other than grief. Examples would be intense anger, guilt, or prior issues that may need individual counselling. Moreover, those who are involved in legal or business matters following the death of a loved one may be too preoccupied to focus on the work involved in the grief process in general and the group work in particular. Lastly, it is advisable to suggest waiting one to two months before joining a group. There is either an initial period of numbness or unreality or there is intense, acute grief requiring individual attention that lasts for this length of time after a death.

The selection and screening process necessitates a pre-group intake session. Following the guidelines in Chapter 2, this session assesses the needs and the functioning of the bereaved and discusses the goals, objectives, and methods used in the support group.

Goals
The goals for this group are to provide an environment that allows and promotes a healthy expression of grief, to increase an awareness and understanding of the broader issues of loss and grief, to educate regarding the process and resolution of grief, to identify effective coping strategies, to facilitate a sense of personal control and decision-making, and to introduce the concepts of memorialization and reinvestment in life.

Session 1: Getting acquainted and goal setting
Open this first session with introductory statements of welcome and acknowledgement of the strength it takes to become part of a group that takes the risk of exploring their grief and sharing it with others who are strangers. State that care will be given to understand and address each member's particular grief and their ability to cope with

it at the present time. Point out that there is no one right way to grieve and that members should not compare themselves with each other or believe that someone else is doing better in their grief work. Encourage members with words that express hope for emotional improvement. Comments can be used such as: 'Tonight everyone is quiet and somewhat fearful. In two to three weeks, there will be talking and laughter among you. As a matter of fact, it will become difficult for me to get your attention. I know that you might find this difficult to believe now; but it will happen.' The letter shared by a member earlier in this chapter can be read at this point for additional encouragement.

Objectives
1. To make preliminary introductions and to discuss group rules, expectations, and the content of each session.
2. To provide an opportunity for members to become acquainted and to learn about the loss (death) of each member.
3. To initiate feelings of universality in the experience of grief.

Interventions
1. Members are asked to introduce themselves and to tell the group something about themselves that is not related to their loss. For example, suggest they tell about their work, areas of interest, or other family members.
2. Group rules, procedures, and expectations (Table 5.1) are discussed. Members are encouraged to express concerns about the procedure, and to clarify their expectations of what will be accomplished within the 10 weeks.
3. Members are matched in dyads based on information obtained during the pre-group intake. Attempts are made to match on perceived similarities of issues related to the loss, age, sex, or personalities. Each person interviews the other, discussing specifics of the loss, feelings then and now, and other areas of difficulty. About 20 to 30 minutes are allowed for this exchange. In the large group, members introduce their partners and the loss that they have experienced. This activity sets the tone for an unthreatening environment, recognizing the pain of grief and the possible difficulty involved in telling a group of strangers about the death. Moreover, it provides an initial opportunity to meet someone who is similar and begins the process of universality and cohesiveness.

Homework Tell members that each week an assignment will be given. They are not forced to do this homework; however, advise

Table 5.1   *Group procedures and expectations*

Confidentiality is expected

Members are encouraged to participate but are not pressured to do so; they may pass.

Co-facilitators are available between meetings.

Homework assignments are given weekly, but are not required to be shared.

The group is supportive in nature, not confrontational.

Others' grief should be left at the meeting, not taken home; each person has enough of his/her own.

The first few meetings may increase the pain and distress of the members; this is normal.

Please attend at least three meetings before you decide to stay or withdraw. If you decide to withdraw, please discuss this with the group leader before withdrawing.

If you cannot attend a session, please call. You are encouraged to attend every session. You are important and the group is not the same when members are absent. Your presence means a lot to everyone and adds support that you may not realize. Everyone is valuable to the group.

We encourage you to share, but we may have to 'move on' sometimes so everyone in the group has an opportunity to talk. Please do not be offended if we have to interrupt.

them that the more effort they put into these 10 weeks and their willingness to take risks, the more they will get from the experience. Explain that the homework is designed to promote thought and reflection on the session just experienced, and also to prepare them for the topic of the next week's session. Explain that grief work is painful and difficult. It is normal upon leaving a session to experience a surge of pain. This will diminish over time, and the early sessions are the most difficult. Invite and encourage members to call you in between the sessions if extra support is needed. Caution them that they should not be alone in their grief.

Ask members to identify three possible goals that they want to accomplish during the 10 weeks. Give guidelines for setting effective goals: simple, not complicated; concrete, not abstract; something to do, not stop doing; self-initiated (i.e. not dependent upon others' help); and immediate (now and not in the future). Examples should be given to illustrate realistic goals that can be set along these guidelines. For example, a goal that states 'I want to feel better in 10 weeks' is too abstract and could be self-defeating. A more specific, concrete, and attainable goal would be one that proposed eating breakfast every day in order to feel better physically. Other possible goals would be to watch the amount of caffeine intake in order to sleep better, to begin daily walking, to get up before noon, or to make one small decision each day in order to regain a sense of personal control.

Discuss the therapeutic value of journal writing and encourage members to begin this type of writing for identification and expression of feelings, and potential growth of self-insight.

Special considerations   The facilitator is relatively directive during this session. Guidelines are set and expectations checked. Members want to know if they will get their needs met in this group. Many start to compare their grief with that of other members. Occasionally, negative judgement will be expressed: 'What is she doing here? I lost my child and she only lost her 95-year-old mother who lived a full life.' If this occurs during the group session, you as the counsellor can choose to ignore it with the understanding that this is normal and that it will change in the next few weeks; or you can address it as it happens within the here-and-now context of the group. You can acknowledge what you have heard and state that this is a normal reaction until members get to know each other better; but validate the feeling and concern that is being expressed. Often reactions such as these are expressed to the counsellor outside the group. In these situations acceptance of such feelings is appropriate, with the acknowledgement that others from past groups have had similar reactions, which change as members become better acquainted. Others become overwhelmed by the grief of another: 'I don't know if I can come back. I hurt so much because of my own grief; I feel that I can't bear hearing about theirs.' For many it is the first time they have verbalized their loss outside the family, and it creates additional discomfort to hear others' loss at the same time. Assure members that these are typical reactions, but that everyone present has the ability to cope with their pain and it is not necessary to take on the additional grief of other members. Tell members that over the next several weeks they will see improvement in each other, and that shared laughter will replace the initial pain and trepidation.

During this first session assess those who may have the tendency to monopolize with their grief or present their grief as more severe and more worthy of attention than others'. The counsellor can encourage members to talk; however, in order to give everyone the same opportunity, you may need to gently interrupt and ask others to contribute.

Another concern during this first session is that members may tend to rationalize their grief as not being as bad as others'. It is not necessary to intervene at this point, but if this becomes a pattern over the sessions you may need to remind members that each person's grief is the most difficult for them and that their grief should not be underestimated. Dependence on rationalization as a defence mechanism allows members to intellectualize the process and avoid experiencing the pain that promotes healing. On other occasions the grief of others may be horrendous. Murders, suicides, and other types of death can be overwhelming to those already burdened with their own grief. Care must be taken to observe and process the initial experience of members as they listen to each other's experiences. Validate the intensity of this first session and assure members that in the course of the 10 weeks, this level of intensity will not persist. Assure members that after the third session there is a shift in focus and affect within the group, and that those who address their grief will experience positive movement in the bereavement process.

Session 2: Understanding the multiple perspectives of grief

Introduce this session with comments that promote an under-standing of the perspectives involved with loss and the tremendous power of grief. Comments should reflect the fact that every aspect of an individual is affected by a loss event; and that one must continue to assess which perspective is emerging at the present time and affecting the bereavement experience. The philosophical, spiritual, psychological, sociological, and physical perspectives can emerge at any time and on multiple occasions during the process. Each time they emerge, there will be different issues to address. For example, the spiritual perspective initially may be influenced by the bereaved's belief that God could have prevented this loss; thus the anger is directed at God. Later on in the process, this perspective may emerge again, with issues of rebuilding a relationship with God.

Objectives
1. To introduce the theme of multiple perspectives of loss.
2. To educate members about the nature and process of grief.
3. To validate and normalize grief behaviours.

Interventions
1. Ask members to share the experience of the first session and process the homework assignment (goals and journal writing). It is important that the group give input to each other regarding goals and possible strategies. At this time it may be necessary to subdivide into groups that represent the same types of loss (e.g. spouse, child). Journal writing is shared for both the content and the affective components. Members begin to relate to each other

as they begin to realize that others share similar feelings and often have the same difficulties coping with everyday living.

2. Refer to your opening comments on the perspectives of loss: significant loss affects one philosophically, spiritually, psychologically, sociologically, and physically (see Chapter 1 for discussion on perspectives). Bereaved individuals do not understand the tremendous power of grief. They feel out of control, and many fear that they are going crazy. A 10-minute presentation to the group regarding these perspectives of grief is important and therapeutic. This information often provides the first ray of hope and reassurance of future resolution. Included in this presentation should be some reference to a model of grief. Any model (Chapter 1) showing the experience of grief as a cyclical process with a resolution phase may be used.

3. Encourage members to share where they are in the grief experience, what has been helpful, and what are they doing to facilitate or hinder the process.

Homework The next session will focus on the therapeutic value of remembering and developing healthy memories of the deceased. Ask members to bring in pictures, items, and memories to share with the group that will allow the group to experience the essence of the lives of the deceased loved ones. A handout, 'Reminiscing', is given (see Table 3.3, p. 55) to encourage meaningful reminiscing. Encourage members to spend time reading this handout and thinking about the many dimensions of the relationship that have been lost through death. Also advise them that it is normal and healthy to have negative as well as positive memories, and that it is helpful in grief resolution to share both. Many need to share the fact that their loved ones had been demanding or self-centred, or that they had annoying habits.

Special considerations Many will have unrealistic goals. The experience of grief is not yet thoroughly understood, and many are hoping for quick solutions and cures from a support group. Pain is still intense during this session, norms are being set, and members are not yet aware of the universality of their grief experience. Structure, direction, and support from the facilitators is important. Many times concrete suggestions will have to be given again to facilitate the goal-setting process.

Session 3: Remembering
Introduce the theme of remembering, using the following as a guideline.

Part of grief resolution entails the development of a realistic memory. Many only remember the best features of an individual or relationship. Others become stuck in the memory of the illness or the death event, which may have been traumatic. And some cannot think of any positive aspects of the deceased's life. In order to emotionally let go (but not forget) and to build a new relationship with the deceased, all the aspects of that individual must be remembered. Remembering, as an active part of the grief work, addresses the need to tell the story of a loved one's life. In this session the group members are encouraged to share pictures, items, or stories (positive and negative) about their loved ones. They describe memories that reflect the fact that we are all human, with human strengths and with frailties that often cause frustration. Through sharing, members allow others into their world. This session is often the pivotal session in which members no longer focus on why their loss is greater or why they are different from one another. Group cohesion and universality should be apparent after this session. If this is not the case, the lack of universality needs to be assessed by the facilitator and addressed with the group.

Others who have had conflicted relationships with the deceased find it difficult to remember anything positive. This can cause a problem in resolution. Unresolved, conflicted relationships foster an excessive focus on negative memories and unfinished business, leading to complications in the grief process. The following illustrates the potential for problems in grief resolution:

> *Female* (aged 35): My mother died seven years ago. I didn't grieve much because I always felt we had a negative relationship. I adored my father, and my mother resented our relationship. I was cleaning things out of their home last year after my father died and I found her diary from when she was a teenager. I realize now I never knew my mother as a person. I also found that she had boxes of everything I ever made, with notes of pride about me on every item. Now I realize that I have to take this journey and go back and learn who my mother was – so I can put the memory of her within me – memories that will bring good feelings – instead of the hatred and anger that I have carried with me.

When memories such as the above are shared, acknowledge the pain being expressed, then focus on the positive that has come out of the process of sharing. Generate support and ideas from the group that will help this woman to find new aspects about her mother. Contacting people who knew her mother might be one way she could learn more about the parent that she did not fully know.

Objectives To develop an appropriate and realistic memory of the deceased and to foster cohesion among members.

Interventions
1. This session draws entirely upon the reminiscences shared by the group. The only educational portion is a few minutes of introduction to the theme of the value of sharing memories, both positive and negative. It is important to recognize that our loved ones were human, with human qualities and frailties. All the memories have to be sorted out and processed. Some who only remember the good memories have a more difficult time of emotionally and cognitively letting go. State that remembering is a valuable component of grief work and helps the bereaved eventually to incorporate their loved ones within them in healthy memory. No one can take away the love that was once experienced, and no one can take away their memories.
2. Invite each member in turn to share pictures, items and memories. For those who have little to share, encourage them to consider some of the questions posed in 'Reminiscing', given to them the previous week to facilitate remembering.

Homework Building on the emotions and issues identified during this session, the homework capitalizes on the need to gain insight into specific feelings and issues that need to be addressed. The assignment is to write a letter to the person who died. The letter can be stream of consciousness or structured to answer questions such as how I felt when you died, how I feel now, what I miss the most, what I do not miss, what I wish I had said or done, and what I wish I had not said or done. The structure allows for exploration of emotions that create conflict in grief resolution. Members are encouraged but not forced to write this letter. They will also be asked if they would like to share the letter or the thoughts and emotions experienced from writing it with the group. With difficult assignments it is helpful to give an example of those in other groups who benefited from this homework, and how. Many have read the entire letter and have felt relief at sharing the burden of ambivalent emotions that they have harboured towards the deceased. Others have shared the fact that they have gained insight into repressed feelings, and now feel relieved or have a better understanding of themselves.

Special considerations The intervention during this session relies greatly upon members' willingness to share meaningful memories with the group. The facilitators, however, must be prepared to generate discussion and move the sharing beyond mere factual reporting if necessary. This is accomplished by attempts to bring individuals into the here and now. This means that the facilitator asks individuals how sharing these memories has made them feel and how this sharing may have raised awareness of deeper issues. Linking, that is, asking other members if they have similar memories or feelings about their loved ones, often promotes cohesiveness and facilitates important connections between members. Another method is to ask members how it felt to share the memories with the group, and ask other members if they have had similar feelings during this session. Those who monopolize should be gently reminded that others need time to share. A possible approach is to say: 'You have some great memories, Ann. Because we still have to hear from others, could you choose your favourite memory to share.' And lastly, if a member has only positive or only negative memories of the deceased, it is necessary to redirect their focus from highly selective memories to an exploration of that person's total life and their relationship with them.

Session 4: Identifying and expressing feelings

To introduce the theme for this session, focus on the need to identify and express all feelings. Explain that avoidance of difficult and painful feelings is one of the common problems associated with grief resolution. In acute phases of grief one feels out of control, and there is a fear of losing more control if feelings are allowed to emerge. Moreover, many do not even know what they are feeling. To facilitate awareness of issues/feelings of commonality, participants are encouraged to share the experience of writing the letter or the reasons for not being able to accomplish the assignment. Once a person can identify specific feelings and acknowledge them and then be provided with an environment for healthy expression, one of the most difficult aspects of grief work has begun. It is a paradox that one can 'lean into the pain' and feel relief and renewed energy. Avoidance depletes energy. Grief work is hard work, and one needs purposeful breaks. However, not to grieve or experience the pain is to deny the healing process and perhaps to complicate it.

The following highlights the benefits experienced by one group member after writing a letter to his deceased father:

A male participant (aged 37) had been referred to the group by his company's psychologist, who believed that current outbursts of anger were somehow related to unresolved issues of his father's death four years ago. In group, he was discussing his experience of writing a letter to his deceased father: 'Last night I was writing this letter on my word processor. I looked up at the screen and couldn't believe it. I was furious with my father. For two months I was the only one who knew he was dying. He wouldn't let me tell anyone, and he wouldn't let me talk to him about his dying. I was the one responsible for his care. He died and I never even got a chance to say the things that I needed to say.'

This member did not read his letter to the group; he was more intent on sharing the experience of writing it and the insight that he had gained into his anger and unresolved grief. It was therapeutic for him to share this experience; the group validated and supported the work he had accomplished through his letter writing. It was also therapeutic for the group as a whole, because those who had avoided writing a letter were able to realize the potential worth of such an exercise.

Objectives   To identify, validate and express painful emotions of grief.

Interventions
1. Ask members to share the experience of writing the letter within the group setting. As indicated from the above example it can have several benefits, both for individual members and for the group as a whole. It builds trust and cohesion, and offers members the opportunity to imitate behaviours that have worked for others. Some choose to read their letters. Often, painful and not previously known feelings are elicited by this assignment, leaving an individual feeling even more overwhelmed. The group offers support by listening and generating suggestions. Most who have shared have expressed a sense of relief or a physical feeling of having a weight removed. There is a saying in bereavement counselling that 'a grief shared is a grief cut in half'.
2. Discuss the nature of feelings for about 15 minutes. A handout called 'Feelings spiral' (Figure 5.1) that shows a variety of emotions can initiate a general discussion. The handout shows the extremes of going from being very 'up' to being very 'down'. Grief has the power to create these swings, and the goal in this process is to move more towards the middle. Members are asked to identify emotions, both positive and negative, and the extremes of them. Discuss the fact that feelings are neither intrinsically good or bad; it is what one does with them that determines if they are positive or negative. Feelings should not be avoided but embraced and worked through.
3. Help members identify the negative and the positive emotions on

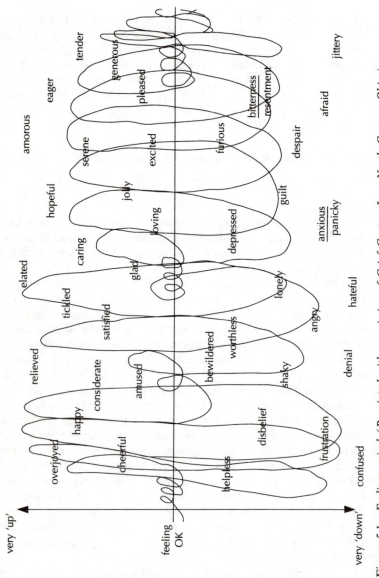

Figure 5.1   *Feelings spiral (Reprinted with permission of Grief Center, Inc., North Canton, Ohio.)*

the handout. Many are only aware of the more unpleasant feelings. Investigate what is occurring when the more pleasant emotions are being experienced. This moves individuals towards empowerment. Many believe that things just happen for no reason at all. Many believe that if they experience a good hour or day, something 'out there' caused it to happen. Once we can facilitate awareness that they are doing something to cause this difference, they can begin to activate behaviours to feel better.

4. Discuss the 'History of loss' (see Chapter 2) and ways that repressed emotion from past losses can be contributing to the present loss and painful emotions. Connect this to the idea that feelings should not be avoided. It is important at this time to help members become aware of and assess past losses; many are often unaware that certain past events have been significant losses in their lives.

Homework Advise members that next week's focus will be on changes made in their lives since the death of their loved one. Discuss the fact that relationships are built over many years, with numerous roles involved. Many do not understand the breadth and depth of grief work, especially as it applies to the many changes and lost roles. Ask members to focus on changes in their lives since the death of their loved ones, and what new roles they have had to assume.

Ask members to complete the 'History of loss' and bring it to the next session. This activity provides additional insight into behavioural and emotional reactions to loss, and allows them to have a clearer understanding of role changes after different losses during their lifetimes. This assignment raises an awareness of the impact of past losses and the effect they have had.

Special considerations When doing the letter assignment for this session, some limit themselves to one or two areas. Others write lengthy letters and desire to read the entire letter to the group to complete the process. Others focus on what was difficult with this assignment, or what they learned about themselves from writing this letter. The assignment is structured, but flexible enough for individuals to use it for their needs and on their timetable. If members have avoided the assignment, encourage them to return to the task when they have more strength.

Session 5: Role changes
Introduce the topic of role changes for about five minutes. The following information and case example can be used.

Bereaved individuals are acutely aware of the physical loss of a person. An important aspect of group work is to address the number of roles or functions that are also lost (i.e. intangible losses) after the death of a significant person. A person is not merely a friend, a child, a parent, or sibling. Relationships provide meaningful roles and are the basis of one's identity. A goal of the session is to help members explore the roles that have been lost or redefined. This is not intended to add more grief or to promote self-pity. It is intended to foster insight into exactly what has been lost (in addition to the actual person) and what needs to be rebuilt. The bereaved are cautioned not to perform all the roles alone; yet they are also cautioned not to realign too quickly. Identities are established over time through the feedback that significant others give regarding roles, strengths, and weaknesses. To reinvest or realign too quickly often negates the opportunity for new aspects of an identity to emerge. Quick replacement is an attractive possibility because it can provide the opportunity to keep busy and avoid the necessary grief work. The ability to learn new skills and to take on new roles allows the bereaved to build self-confidence and regain a sense of personal control:

> I finally figured out how to use the weedwhacker; then I decided to redo the living room. He was always busy working and never showed me how to do anything. He handled all the important things. He said a woman didn't have to know how to do these things. (57-year-old widow)

An example such as the above is indicative of responses given by members as they begin to understand the meaning of role change in their lives. Others may need more help to develop insight into these changes and support to initiate new behaviours. The group can be an excellent resource for generating ideas and offering opportunities for needed behaviour changes.

Objectives
1. To discuss and process the 'History of loss' in order to gain insight into the effects of past loss and change on the present loss.
2. To understand the multifaceted nature of loss as it affects roles and identity.
3. To explore healthy role realignments.

Interventions
1. Ask members to share their 'History of loss'. They can share specific losses, general reactions or styles of coping, multiple

changes endured throughout the years because of these losses, or how the past is affecting the present experience. In addition to the awareness and insight that this activity generates, it also provides a framework for designing interventions. For example, an individual may learn that he or she has had multiple losses and that the way of coping had always been to avoid pain and to quickly replace what had been lost. As this individual now faces role changes after the death of a significant person, the tendency might be to try to replace this person quickly and have others take over the roles that had been provided by the deceased. This awareness leads to designing interventions that help this individual stop inappropriate past patterns of response to loss, and develop new ways of coping.

2. Initiate an activity that will visually demonstrate role losses and changes. The paper plate activity (Figure 5.2) can be used. Members are given paper plates, markers, and scissors. They are instructed to think back six months to a year before their loved ones died and to consider what roles they were involved in with them, and what percentage of their time was involved in each role. Many put down roles of caretaker, spouse, parent, church member, and so on. They are then instructed to cut out the roles that are no longer there or have changed. Many cut out the role of spouse and caretaker, and are left with a wedge that represents 20 per cent of remaining roles in their lives. Others also cut out pieces from church and parental roles, if this had been a shared role. This heightens awareness of the voids in their lives, and gives expression to feelings of aloneness and emptiness, not thoroughly understood before this exercise.

3. Encourage members to share insights regarding changes, especially in terms of roles and identity.

4. Get input within the group regarding new roles that they have assumed since the death.

5. Discuss the need to have meaningful roles in life and the necessity to begin to think of new roles (not replacements). Roles are purposively chosen to give one a sense of identity. Replacements are not thought through; instead a person or an activity is quickly chosen to fill the void that one feels after the death of a loved one.

Homework As members explore past and present losses, significant role changes, and the emotional impact on their lives as a result, they become more acutely aware of the stress they are experiencing. This session has begun the process of a more in-depth investigation into change, and the stress created by change. The next session will

Activity to facilitate an understanding of role changes after loss

Instructions:
1.   Discuss the fact that a death (or other losses) includes the loss of various roles. Understanding these past roles facilitates an awareness of the impact of the loss event, the voids that have been created, and the necessity to consider realignment of roles in the future.

2.   Encourage members to evaluate what roles have been lost: however, warn them not to quickly attempt to replace the voids. Moreover, advise them not to be forced by others to take on roles just to occupy their time.

3.   Distribute the paper plates, markers, and scissors. Instruct them to think back six months before the death and to consider the roles that they were involved in, noting the percentage of time for each role (give examples).

4.   Instruct members to create pie-shaped wedges (various sizes) that represent roles and the percentage of time involved. Next instruct them to cut out roles or portions of roles that no longer exist because of the death (loss). For example one might still be a parent; however, that role has been reduced because it might have been a shared role. Thus a percentage of that role must be cut out.

5.   Upon completion, instruct members to share with the group their plate, explaining what has been lost or changed.

The following is an example presented by a bereaved father, following the death of his 16-year-old daughter. Although he had four surviving children, a wife, a profession, and was actively involved in the community, this exercise provided a visual representation that promoted insight into present feelings of turmoil, fragmentation, and disorganization. Using the input from the group as this activity was processed, he was able to focus on potential strategies to address varied emotions and to consider role realignments.

Roles identified six months prior

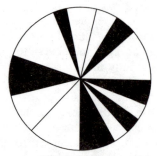

Roles – Present
Pieces of every role had to be
eliminated, leaving fragments

The shaded areas represent segments he had to eliminate. Although he still had a portion of these roles, he became acutely aware of the involvement he and his daughter had in each other's lives. He was a leader in her church youth group, employed her during the summer, attended her sport functions, and participated with her in a number of community activities.

Figure 5.2   *Paper plate exercise*

help members understand the connection between grief, change, and additional stress. It is the intent of these sessions to help members break behaviours, thoughts, and emotions down into smaller components, thus making them more workable. This week's assignment is to write about specific events or personal situations that upset the writer during the week, and how he or she resolved them. The purpose of the assignment is for each person to identify stressors and ways of coping, which will then be reviewed during the next session.

Special considerations The paper plate activity facilitates group cohesion and universality. Members visually understand that they are sharing a common experience. Many of these role changes have not been prepared for, such as the widower who has to cook and do the laundry, or the widow who has to make decisions about the house. Another important feature of this session is the insight gained regarding the multifaceted nature of roles. Many do not understand the diversity of roles and the relationships involved, and try to replace the missing 'role' with a new 'wife', 'child', 'friend', and so forth.

Session 6: Stress

Introduce the topic of stress for about five minutes. The following may be used as a brief introduction, supplemented by any additional information on the topic that the counsellor believes to be pertinent to the particular group. For example, if the group contains widows who are mothers, acknowledgement of their particular type of stress (raising children/adolescents as single parents) may be appropriate.

Stress is a normal part of everyday life. Loss and grief bring additional stress. Some may only have a vague idea that they are 'stressed out'. Within the group it is helpful to identify specific stressors, when they occur, how often, how they have been dealt with, and specific healthier ways of coping.

Examine stress on three different levels: affective, cognitive, and behavioural. On the behavioural level, it is important to assess the stress that is accrued from doing too much or doing nothing at all. Often the grief experience is overwhelming because it involves an enormous amount of non-grief work, such as paperwork and legal problems:

> I took care of my mother for the last ten years. After my divorce 30 years ago, she became my life, and I gave most of my time and energy to her. For the last two years of my life she lived in my home and I physically took care of her and became responsible for all her needs and business affairs. I also continued to rent two

houses during all this time. I have months of paperwork on my desk. The pile continues to increase, yet I have no motivation to do anything about it. I think I am stressed because of so much to do, and stressed because I am not doing anything. (64-year-old woman following the death of her mother)

An appropriate intervention in a situation such as the above would be to initiate a plan to take care of the volumes of paperwork. The plan needs to address the task in manageable components, as the individual is already overwhelmed by the thought and sight of the task that needs to be accomplished on top of already being mentally preoccupied and stressed beyond her endurance.

Objectives   To discuss the fact that there was stress before the death and that specific issues and feelings of grief increase stress. Many aspects of grief must go through a process that cannot be rushed; however, resolution in areas of stress can be beneficial. Often this is one of the few areas in which the bereaved can gain some control and set realistic goals. Relief of stress is an empowering factor that initiates feelings of personal control.

Interventions
1. Ask members to share the homework regarding what was stressful last week and how it was handled. Generate discussion based on what was learned from the situation, what they did that was helpful, and what needs to be altered.
2. Discuss (for about 10 minutes) stress in more detail, incorporating ideas from the introduction to this session. Use any current information on the nature and effect of stress on the human body.
3. Give members the handouts that allow them to identify and assess areas and levels of stress, and to sort out those which are important/not important and controllable/not controllable (Tables 5.2 and 5.3). Promote discussion from members, based on the information presented and the handouts. Put responses on a chalkboard or a paper chart. Work towards helping members let go of stressors that are not important and to find solutions, even partial solutions.

Homework   The next session will build on this one. Coping styles will be examined in more depth, and new possibilities for coping will be presented. Ask members to fill out a 'coping inventory' (Table 5.4). Coping inventories offer a wide variety of coping styles. They help individuals see negative ways they might be coping and open

Table 5.2 *Levels of stress*

I.	Emotional level:	Feelings of anxiety, nervous, panic, can't concentrate, go blank.
	Coping behaviours:	Relaxation techniques Breathing exercises Meditation Prayer Imagery Music Physical exercise Healthy expression of feelings
II.	Thinking level:	Beliefs reflect 'shoulds', 'musts', 'oughts'. Inaccurate appraisal of situations. Lack of confidence in coping abilities.
	Coping behaviours:	Rethink and change perceptions, beliefs, and self-statements. Get accurate information about events and examine possible and plausible interpretations of an event. Develop communication skills. Get assertiveness training.
III.	Behavioural level:	Stress can be caused by what you are doing or not doing (e.g. putting things off, acting before thinking).
	Coping behaviours:	Evaluate what you are doing. Change what you are doing. Make other choices. Re-evaluate, prioritize, make new plans. Learn new skills.

Table 5.3 *Stressors*

Stressors that are important		Stressors that aren't important	
controllable	uncontrollable	controllable	uncontrollable
1. Lack of things to do	Family is not supportive	Allow phone calls to go unanswered	rain/snow
2.			
3.			
4.			
5.			

Stressors that are important and that we can control need to be worked on. Those that are unimportant and under our control can be either dealt with or ignored. Stressors that are either important or unimportant and out of our control should be let go of, as there is nothing that can be done about the uncontrollable stressors in your life. *Concentrate on the ones that are under your control.*

Table 5.4   *Coping behaviours*

The following identifies a number of ways different individuals cope with stress in their lives. They represent positive and negative ways of addressing life's challenges. Often we depend on one or just a few ways of dealing with stress. Some situations demand additional coping skills or new approaches. Read the following and rate how likely you are to use the different behaviours. Then reflect on whether or not it is effective in every situation, whether it is helping you or creating additional stress, and what new ones from this list might be effective.

> 1 = Never
> 2 = Seldom
> 3 = Sometimes
> 4 = Usually
> 5 = Always

1. Use drugs (nonprescription) or alcohol	1	2	3	4	5
2. Talk with others	1	2	3	4	5
3. Learn as much as possible about the situation	1	2	3	4	5
4. Keep so busy that you don't have time to think	1	2	3	4	5
5. Overeat	1	2	3	4	5
6. Miss meals/eat sporadically	1	2	3	4	5
7. Exercise	1	2	3	4	5
8. Use humour as a release	1	2	3	4	5
9. Ventilate through tears	1	2	3	4	5
10. Try to forget	1	2	3	4	5
11. Turn it over to God	1	2	3	4	5
12. Find solace in nature	1	2	3	4	5
13. Listen to music	1	2	3	4	5
14. Make new choices	1	2	3	4	5
15. Take on new roles	1	2	3	4	5
16. Get medical help	1	2	3	4	5
17. Take more rests	1	2	3	4	5
18. Get a massage	1	2	3	4	5
19. Learn relaxation techniques	1	2	3	4	5
20. Meditate	1	2	3	4	5
21. Find good in the issue/problem	1	2	3	4	5
22. Rename the problem to make it solvable	1	2	3	4	5
23. Hope for relief	1	2	3	4	5
24. Get others' input for solutions	1	2	3	4	5
25. Take a trip	1	2	3	4	5
26. Keep a journal/write letters, etc.	1	2	3	4	5
27. Take care of unfinished business	1	2	3	4	5
28. Repress emotions	1	2	3	4	5
29. Treat yourself as you would a friend	1	2	3	4	5
30. Drive fast to let tensions out	1	2	3	4	5
31. Immerse yourself in work/hobby	1	2	3	4	5
32. Seek solace within church activities	1	2	3	4	5
33. Shout, scream, bang doors, curse	1	2	3	4	5
34. Make a plan to do something (take action)	1	2	3	4	5
35. Accept it as unfair and let it go	1	2	3	4	5

Table 5.4   *(Continued)*

36. Reflect on ways past problems were coped with	1	2	3	4	5
37. Wait for a miracle	1	2	3	4	5
38. Act quickly (without thinking)	1	2	3	4	5
39. Take others' advice	1	2	3	4	5
40. Move – start over	1	2	3	4	5

up potential ways of coping. Present the idea that inability to cope at this time is not a sign of weakness. Past, effective coping strategies may not work in new situations. This exercise provides the opportunity to personally evaluate what still works, what is not effective, and what new strategies can be added.

Special considerations   This session is practical and is pivotal in facilitating awareness of specific stressors and potential solutions. In terms of the tasks of grief, it provides the opportunity to adjust to an environment that is different because of the loss. The ability to make new choices and to take some action provides a basis for rebuilding a future existence.

Session 7: Coping (including coping with holidays, birthdays, special events)

Introduce the theme of coping as an active response to loss. Coping includes the ideas of accommodation and assimilation. As individuals relearn their worlds after loss, new information about themselves and their environments must be assimilated. The bereaved strive to somehow maintain the essence of their identities, yet adapt to new lives and environments. Coping involves identifying specific stressors and understanding what needs to be altered. Changes often have to be made in present coping styles. Options for coping are discussed in the group, ideas shared, and specific strategies are explored for each level (affective, cognitive, and behavioural) of stress.

Specifically, holidays and special events are highlighted as intense periods of stress and potential emotional pain. They cannot be avoided, and they need to be carefully planned. Holidays and special events have the potential to arouse a multitude of past memories, many very painful. Planning with other family members can be instrumental in avoiding unnecessary grief:

I knew Christmas was going to be hard. This will be our first one since my husband died. So I called together my two daughters and we decided how we were going to cope with the actual day. We decided that giving gifts would be OK. However, we will exchange gifts the night before and not wrap them. We all agreed that unwrapping them would be too difficult. (55-year-old widow)

The above represents a typical response after permission is given within the group to alter traditions for celebrating holidays and special events. Individuals have solutions within them; most have not been given permission to express them or to act upon them.

Objectives
1. To identify coping strategies that help facilitate the grief process.
2. To identify time periods that create stress, e.g. holidays and anniversaries, and specific coping strategies for them.

Interventions
1. Discuss the homework regarding coping strategies. Are present ones effective? Explore specific areas of coping: mental, spiritual, physical, behavioural, and emotional. What specific ways do members have of coping in each of these areas?
2. Discuss the potential of holidays, anniversaries, and other events to elicit pain.
3. When appropriate, ask members to share plans and concerns about anticipated events or seasons.

Homework   Next week's session focuses on another active part of bereavement: memorializing or commemorating. In grief, one feels that everything is out of control. Memorialization, especially through the creation of rituals, promotes awareness of some personal control again. Ask members to identify what has been done to commemorate or memorialize their loved ones. Encourage them to commemorate beyond the funeral ritual. Most do not understand the therapeutic value of remembering or memorializing after the funeral rite. Suggest that they consider what was of value or meaning to their loved ones, and how this could be memorialized in a meaningful way. Give some basic ideas such as contributing to a charity or developing a scholarship fund in the name of the deceased.

Special considerations   This session has the potential to be helpful, from day-to-day coping to coping with major holidays and events. Many realize during this session that they are having difficulty because they continue to use strategies that may have been effective in the past, but currently are not useful. It is often a relief to learn that it is not personal deficits or weaknesses that are causing coping difficulties. Most members are willing to try new behaviours at this point, and can usually select new strategies from the coping inventory or from each other.

Session 8: Memorialization/commemoration and therapeutic use of rituals

For this introduction connect the theme of memorialization back to the theme of remembering in the third session. Memorialization implies a more active process, as it requires some action on the part of the bereaved. Memorializion begins with the funeral rite and can continue for an indefinite period of time. The goal is to incorporate a loved one in healthy memory and to reinvest in meaningful life. Not to invest in life again would negate the meaning of the life of a loved one.

Rituals (Rando, 1988) can be utilized to facilitate memorialization. During this group session, members learn about the relationship between rituals, tasks of grief, and grief resolution. They are encouraged to begin to identify where they are in the process and tasks of grief, and to explore possibilities for personal rituals.

The behaviour (ritual) is designed to express internal feelings of grief in order that others may better understand the depth and nature of the grief. A ritual may be done once, as in the ritual of the funeral; or it may be repeated. A ritual is structured and has a time limit. Family and friends may be more willing to participate if they understand exactly what is expected of them, and that there is an end point. Often supporters abandon the bereaved because they tire of endless grief, and they do not know what to do to help. Rituals provide a framework and a channel for emotional energy. They facilitate grieving and resolution.

Using the 'Experiences of grief' (see Table 2.6, p. 38), it is possible to design a ritual to facilitate expression and movement at any point in the process. Examples are as follows:

To experience the risk of exploration, understanding, and cognitive acceptance Those who do not talk about the loss or address it in some manner may avoid it and can deny that it has occurred. Often cognitive acceptance can take a year, as the 'firsts' for everything (holidays, seasons, etc.) have to be experienced in order to accept the reality that this death/loss has happened. Many people refuse to change anything in their environment because change challenges and breaks through denial. An illustration of this resistance and denial follows.

A young widow (aged 29) discussed the long-term process of her husband's chemotherapy treatment for cancer. The chemotherapy had been administered at a hospital, located over an hour from their home. The night before she left for this scheduled visit, she had made a pot of lentil soup that he had always enjoyed upon his return. He died, unexpectedly, during this stay. Three months had passed since his death and the covered pot of soup remained on the top shelf of the refrigerator. Every time she opened the refrigerator, a small part of her continued to say that he was alive in the hospital. She came to realize that this was an unconscious strategy that allowed her to deny the reality of his death. Moreover, she came to realize that this denial was preventing her grief work. An important ritual was the elimination of the soup. This was accomplished, but not without pain. The reality that he would never return was accepted.

To fully experience all dimensions of pain: psychologically, spiritually, cognitively, emotionally, and physically It is difficult to conceptualize the notion that if one embraces the pain the grief becomes more bearable. Rituals can be designed at this part of the process to assist the bereaved to take the risks that will incur additional pain. After the third session of the support group, the assignment was to write a letter to the person who had died. This type of writing is a structured ritual intended to facilitate the identification and healthy expression of emotions.

Here is another example of this type of ritual. A bereaved mother whose son committed suicide invited her remaining three adult children together for a short prayer service and a meal. She designed invitations that instructed them to bring a covered dish that represented a favourite food that they had shared as children, and the memory of an occasion shared together. They were also asked to bring a meaningful reading to share in a short prayer service before dinner. This ritual addressed the reality of the suicide; yet it also celebrated a life that had been lived. Often in violent deaths, the bereaved cannot remember anything except the horror of the death. Rituals such as these encourage remembrance of a total life, not just the end. Without the ability to remember and memorialize the whole person, one can become stuck in unresolved grief.

To experience the present environment that is a poignant reminder of the loss An environment is everything. It is a place, a time, a memory, a song, a food, a season, a person, and so forth. The environment is present and constant. A ritual that facilitates task work within the concept of the environment is an attempt to gain a sense of what you can control. Denying, avoiding, or leaving things to chance only allows for continued feelings of grief and loss of control. Here is an example of a ritual to address the task of adjusting to the environment.

> Christmas was approaching. No one had discussed how the day would be handled. As the day grew nearer and plans were made for the dinner, it became obvious that no one wanted to sit in Dad's chair. Should we remove it? The space would make his absence clear to us. Then Joe had an idea: why not invite Bess over for dinner? She was elderly and lived alone, and her children were out of state.

Filling the empty chair is a task that many face during their first holidays. Taking an active stance and planning restores some sense of personal control. Moreover, the 'ritual' of filling the empty chair also provides an opportunity for altruism, another healing factor in the grief process.

To experience integration of the loss experience and to reinvest in meaningful living   Reinvestment in life does not mean forgetting or ceasing to actively remember the deceased. Loved ones will always be a part of us. The highest form of memorializing is to live a meaningful life as a tribute to the deceased. Any behaviour done in memory and with the purpose of reinvesting is a ritual. The therapeutic aspect of a ritual is that it empowers you to act upon the world. To symbolize this power to rebuild and reinvest, many choose an item as a ritual that signifies new life. Garden plants are frequently chosen as symbolic reinvestments in life.

Objectives
1. To understand the therapeutic properties of rituals.
2. To consider memorialization as an ongoing part of the grief experience.
3. To begin the process of active reinvestment.

Interventions
1. Introduce the concept of memorialization. Process the homework assignment. Encourage sharing ideas of what has been done and future intentions to commemorate loved ones.
2. Discuss the relationship of rituals to memorialization and healthy resolution for about 5 to 10 minutes. (Use information and examples from the opening comments for this session.)
3. Encourage the sharing of ideas of possible personal rituals and rituals already enacted to facilitate the grief process. (Many have experiences to share that may not have been recognized or integrated as therapeutic rituals.)

Homework   Discuss the need for ongoing support systems and the need to identify the people who are at present providing needed support.

Discuss the idea that some healing can be attained by helping others. Ask members to reach out and support someone who is experiencing a difficult time this week (e.g. by greeting card, phone call, visit), and to process the feelings they experience afterwards in their written journals.

Distribute the psychological needs assessment and planning sheet (Table 3.4, p. 58). This tool was discussed in Chapters 2 and 3.

Advise members that there are two sessions left. Ask if there are any unanswered questions or new issues.

Special considerations   The notion of rituals is usually well received by the group. Once explained, it is not a difficult concept to grasp. It provides the opportunity to take some action, instead of constantly feeling acted upon by external forces. Many have already enacted rituals without realizing it.

Session 9: Assessing support systems and rebuilding and relearning the world

Introduce this week's theme by connecting it to the homework assignment. Bereaved individuals need to give and receive support. Giving support to those who are also in pain or experiencing difficulties is a form of altruism, which facilitates personal healing and resolution. Receiving support is also an integral part of the bereavement and healing processes. It is important to assess what is currently available, and determine if these systems are effective. Supportive friends and family can give uninformed and unhelpful advice, or only tell the bereaved what they think they (the bereaved) want to hear. Often the most useful support is to tell someone that what he or she is at present doing could be harmful to his or her future well-being. This type of support is difficult to give to bereaved individuals because no one wants to cause additional pain.

Support is needed in many different ways over the course of bereavement. Without good support systems the grieving process is even more difficult. As the bereaved move from the acute phases of grief, they are often in a position to help support others. It can be noted that helping others is itself healing – the helper becomes helped. This effort often complements the grief process and begins the next phase of rebuilding. Rebuilding and relearning one's world cannot come before the pain of grief is fully experienced; yet many try to rush through this as if it were another 'daily' task to be accomplished. This is an active process that implies accommodation and assimilation. The goal is for the bereaved to regain a sense of empowerment and control. The phrase 'relearning the world' (Attig, 1992) connotes positive outcomes to a negative experience.

Assessing support systems and beginning the process of rebuilding necessitates an evaluation of what has changed and what one still has. Rebuilding is based on what remains (i.e. what has not been lost through this experience).

Objectives
1. To assess present support systems and to understand the value of altruism in the healing process.
2. To understand what has changed, yet comprehend what is still intact and meeting psychological needs.
3. To begin the process of making new choices and rebuilding a new identity.
4. To understand the therapeutic function of hope.

Interventions
1. Inquire if any members have unanswered questions or new issues that have emerged. Allow time to answer questions. If new issues have emerged, assess whether or not they can be addressed within the context of the group, or if individual counselling would be more appropriate.
2. Process the assignment regarding support systems. Introduce the concept of healing through altruism and the potential each member has to support another bereaved individual. If members do not have support systems beyond this group, use group time to help identify potential support systems. Many members will offer support to each other when they become aware of the needs of others.
3. Process the assignment regarding psychological needs. Involve the group in helping each other identify future choices in the different areas of 'need'. Brainstorming techniques generate valid ideas to consider.

Homework   Remind members that next week is the final week and that the focus will be on evaluation of the 10 weeks and on positives. Ask members to think about one personal change experienced during the 10 weeks and be prepared to share it.

Instruct them to be prepared to tell each member one positive change that they have observed about each other during the last 10 weeks.

Ask them to think about their own uniqueness and gifts. Remind them that in session 3, items, pictures, and stories were shared to show the beauty of their loved ones' lives. This next session will honour and celebrate their own lives. In our experience, some members have brought in items that they have created. One member brought in several quilts she had made. Another brought in his band instrument from 1923, and several music instruction books that he had written during his professional career. One man talked about his ability to cook and invited everyone over for a special dinner. A retired art teacher offered free art lessons to everyone in the group. As this request is made, it is wise to share examples such as these, since the assignment can be confusing.

Ask members if they would like to bring light refreshments the next week as part of the closure and celebration of life. If so, make arrangements at the end of this session.

Special considerations   Through the processing of individuals' psychological needs assessments, this session provides insight into what has not been lost through death. Many are surprised what still remains and the options available for new choices. In addition, this session addresses the need to give and receive support. There will always be members who have little support available and little left to rebuild upon. It has been our experience, however, that as other members become aware of this, they readily offer support in various ways.

Session 10: Closure/celebration of life
Open this session with statements of appreciation for each member and the risks that they have taken to share their pain with each other. Validate the fact that you have observed growth and change in everyone over the past 10 weeks. Acknowledge the fact that today is the formal end of this group and that this often brings up additional feelings of loss and grief. Share the fact that many in the past have chosen to continue to meet informally and have benefited from ongoing mutual support.

Objectives
1. To identify change and growth.
2. To share a unique aspect of self and to promote the idea of celebrating life.
3. To acknowledge the need for continued support as the 'formal' group terminates. Inquire if any members have unanswered questions. Allow time to answer questions. If new issues have emerged, assess whether or not they can be addressed within the context of the group, or if individual counselling would be more appropriate.
4. To evaluate the experience and bring closure.

Table 5.5 *Evaluation*

Think about your experience in this group. Please respond in the most honest way possible to the items below. This will be kept confidential. Do not be concerned if you have some negative feelings; people sometimes do and are hesitant to say so.

The responses are **Definitely yes, Yes, Unsure, No**, and **Definitely not**. In addition to a response, please give some specifics regarding your experience and opinions.

1. In general, did you make good progress?
2. Do you feel that the group leader (counsellor) had a good understanding of you and your individual issues?
3. Do you feel that you were clear about what you wanted to accomplish in this group within the number of sessions (goals)?
4. Were there certain things that you were afraid to share with the group leader or the group? If so, do you wish to indicate anything at this time that was/is a concern for you?
5. Are you handling things better now than before the group began?
6. Do you feel that you learned things about yourself? If so, what?
7 Do you feel that the group leader shared with you all the information that you needed in order to cope better with your issues?
8. Please list things that worked best for you during the course of the 10 weeks of the group sessions:
9. Please indicate things that did not work for you:
10. Did you feel that you were able to connect to and relate with others in the group?

Interventions

1. Ask each member to fill out an evaluation form regarding the group experience (Table 5.5). Address any unanswered questions and recommend individual counselling for those who have additional issues that cannot be satisfactorily handled during this last session.
2. Encourage members to express their own change and growth and to share insights regarding other members' change and growth.
3. Ask members to share stories, pictures, or items that they have brought that will allow the group to experience a special part of who they are.
4. If food has been brought, allow time for this celebration of life as a way to formally close the ten weeks.

Special considerations The final session represents another loss in the lives of those already coping with loss through death. Attention must be given to this, and it must be processed in the here-and-now setting of this final session. Encourage members to share how they feel about the fact that this is the last session. Move this towards a discussion of coping strategies and continued support of one another. Most groups will appoint someone to organize future sessions together. It is not always the entire group that remains together, but some portion of the group is likely to continue.

Groups will always mirror some part of each member's private reality and offer an opportunity to practise change that needs to be accomplished outside of the therapeutic setting. It has been our experience that the 'power of the group experience' brings issues to awareness sooner than in individual counselling and provides an appropriate environment in which to practise behaviours, gain needed support, and more expediently facilitate the full experience of grief.

6

Anticipatory Grief

Anticipatory grief is a term that is most often associated with a terminal illness, with a prognosis of impending death within a stated time period. However, anticipatory grief can refer to a process for any loss that is expected in the future. Many illnesses that are not terminal have characteristics of large-scale change for the individuals and others involved with them. Heart disease, arthritis, and cancer are only a few of the medical conditions that alter lifestyles and involve significant personal losses. Moving, job changes, and retirement are also significant losses that are not often recognized as such, but require anticipatory work. The list is extensive; and as mentioned in Chapter 1, losses occur from the time one is born until one dies. Many of these losses could be more satisfactorily resolved if time was spent understanding what has already changed and anticipating what is going to be lost, what the potential effects of this loss are, and what one might do to prepare for this event. Anticipatory grief does not mean that one can avoid the pain of grief after a loss; it means that the defences can somehow be better prepared to cope with the full bereavement experience. Without an awareness of a future loss or preparation for it, individuals are more likely to feel as if they have been assaulted and experience being out of control.

Definitions and conceptions

Rando (1986) discussed the fact that there are no precise and consistent definitions of this type of grief. Acknowledging this, she first outlined what it is not. One error is to assume that because a person is terminally ill, anticipatory grief is present. Many patients and families in programmes and institutions for the terminally ill continue to deny the impending death or to hope that a recovery might yet be possible. Another is that anticipatory grief is post-death grief begun earlier, or that there is a fixed volume of grief to be experienced and that anticipatory grief will reduce the amount that has to be experienced after the loss. Findings from Glick, Weiss, and Parkes (1974) have confirmed that grief after an unanticipated loss differs in form and duration from grief for one that is anticipated.

The reason is that a loss that is unexpected has the potential to overwhelm the individual's ability to adapt, thus affecting the ability to function and recover. With sudden loss, the bereaved are often left on their own to understand what has happened to them. Individuals express more anxiety and lack of personal control when they have had no time to prepare. Many express spending longer in a state of shock, and remember the need to retell the event several times, in order to reconstruct it and attempt to make some sense of it. Lastly, there are more expressions of preventability and feelings of guilt, i.e. belief that one could have done something to prevent it if one had only known about it. A common reaction by family members after a death following a heart attack is that they could have called an ambulance and saved the person if only they had been there at the right time.

With anticipatory grief, the time factor involved is an important variable. Lack of time to prepare adequately or too much time to anticipate can also be unproductive. Rando's (1983) study with parents whose children died of cancer showed that less than six months did not allow enough time to prepare, and longer than 18 months resulted in an experience that compromised and depleted the parents' abilities to cope with the illness and the demands of being caretakers.

Rando (1986) acknowledged the difficulty of defining anticipatory grief. One reason for this difficulty is that previous researchers have viewed this concept as being unitary and evolving in a linear fashion. She views it in a multidimensional way and conceives the processes across two perspectives, three time foci, and three classes of influencing variables. The various processes of anticipatory grief are defined as

> the phenomenon encompassing the processes of mourning, coping, interaction, planning, and psychosocial reorganization that are stimulated and begun in part in response to the awareness of the impending loss of a loved one and the recognition of associated losses in the past, present, and future. It is seldom explicitly recognized, but the truly therapeutic experience of anticipatory grief mandates a delicate balance among the mutually conflicting demands of simultaneously holding onto, letting go of, and drawing closer to the dying patient. (1986: 24)

The two perspectives are the dying patient and the family or those emotionally close to the dying patient. For each, the experience will be somewhat different.

The three time foci that Rando (1986) uses demonstrate that the grief is not just for a future event; it includes part of the past which has had to have been let go of, and the present which involves ongoing chances to grieve. Lastly, the influencing variables on the experience involve psychological, emotional, and physiological components.

For those who are emotionally involved with a dying person, the process is demanding, with conflicting pulls. Rando (1986) described this conflict as simultaneously having to come to terms with the prognosis both cognitively and affectively; staying involved with the dying person on a daily basis; and addressing family reorganization issues, which requires adaptation to new roles and responsibilities. Many who have difficulty managing these processes and coping with the time foci and interrelated variables attempt to disengage emotionally from the dying person while he or she is still alive. This premature emotional disengagement has negative effects both on the patient and after the death on the bereaved, who must come to terms with guilt and other difficult emotions.

Issues related to anticipated losses other than impending death

As discussed at the beginning of this chapter, there are many other types of loss that necessitate a process of anticipation and sadness for some part of life that is changing and for a future that might be less meaningful or rich because of loss and change. Gestalt theory addresses this need to pay attention to that which is changing and to grieve it before the new can be embraced. Grief is one of the primary emotions within Gestalt theory, as it is viewed as 'the emotion necessary to the process of destructuring within the gestalt cycle. Grief is necessary to living, as it is the emotional reaction to the losses we know during times of change' (Clark, 1985: 50).

Consider the example of retirement. Most people plan when they will retire; however, often little is done to anticipate this event as a major loss of roles and identity in their lives. Often these individuals never seek counselling, but those who do reflect unresolved issues, psychosomatic and psychiatric symptoms, and an inability to reinvest in meaningful living.

Coping with illness, especially chronic or life-threatening, has several aspects of loss to address, including one's eventual mortality. Even before a medical diagnosis is made, individuals have experienced some unwanted changes in their lives. After the diagnosis, the prognosis often includes physical, mental, and other lifestyle changes that need to be anticipated and prepared for. For those who have heart disease, the underlying grief is the fact that the heart is no longer reliable. When the heart can no longer be depended upon to perform its function, it is a loss experience that needs to be grieved in order to reinvest in meaningful living. This includes grieving for the loss of functioning, but also includes anticipatory grief for necessary changes that accompany heart disease. However, what often happens is stubbornness and denial, in the form of holding fast to former lifestyles, with a determination to prove that nothing has changed. Anticipatory grief would serve to address normal emotions that need validation and expression, and to help plan for future changes, with individuals participating in decision-making for alternative choices. As with other losses, life will never be the same again, and how one viewed oneself needs to be changed. This cannot occur in a linear manner. As with other issues that necessitate a bereavement experience, coping with heart disease is a cyclical process that often involves setbacks.

Models of intervention

Hospice programmes are among the most widely known approaches to caring for dying patients and those who will be involved with them during their last days. This movement originated in St Joseph's Hospital in London in the 1950s, addressing the right to die and the need to offer palliative care to the terminally ill. Dr Cecily Saunders founded St Christopher's Hospice in 1968, and this became the model used to initiate the hospice movement worldwide (Rando, 1986).

In the United States individuals are eligible for hospice when a prognosis has been determined that cure is no longer possible, and that there are six months or less to live. Hospice care is palliative, with pain control as a primary goal of medical intervention. In addition to the medical professionals, a hospice programme usually includes a team of mental health caregivers: counsellors, social workers, clergy, and volunteers for respite care. Most hospice care programmes in the United States take place within the home environment of the patient and family. At least one person must assume the responsibility of being the primary caretaker. Some programmes also have physical facilities for the patient and family members. Hospice programmes vary, and often services offered depend upon local resources and funding and reimbursement from third parties. Their philosophy is rooted in the belief that a person is important until he or she dies, and that there is still life to be lived in a quality manner. In its ideal form, the intention is for the patient to be given voice in his or her treatment within the home environment.

Corr (1991) proposed four primary dimensions of personhood: physical, psychological, social, and spiritual. The physical dimensions of hospice care are usually addressed by the medical staff, with the other helping professions (clergy, counsellors, and social workers) intervening for the last three. Discussing the psychological tasks, Corr emphasized the importance of maximizing the psychological security, autonomy and richness of living one's life, and being in control as much as possible. Among the social tasks is the need to sustain and enhance the interpersonal attachments which are significant to the dying person. Many do not understand that there are a number of social implications of dying. The dying person has had life membership of his or her social environment; thus dying should not take place in isolation. Society often does not recognize the dying. Their names may be dropped from conversations before they die. They have lost their past roles in that society; so society does not know what to do with them in this final process of living. Professionals may need to be advocates to facilitate the integration of the dying person with his or her social environment.

Spiritually, it is important to identify, develop, or reaffirm sources of spiritual energy, and in doing so foster hope for some type of continued (though compromised) meaning in this life, and some type of existence after physical life has ended. Corr's approach is to assess a patient and those involved, determine areas of task work (based on the four dimensions of personhood), and design interventions based on the assessment. His model emphasizes the need for professional caregivers of every discipline to enhance their understanding of their patients as unique individuals, to foster empowerment on the part of the patients, to emphasize participation (i.e. shared aspects of dying that require interpersonal communication and interactions with others), and to guide helping (i.e. professionals should not dictate treatment plans).

Whatever intervention model is used, it must address the patients and those involved, and understand ways of effectively supporting and intervening. Many professionals, especially the medically oriented ones, direct attention towards physical cures. Using the 'Perspectives' (Chapters 1 and 2) allows for more in-depth assessment, resulting in more effective treatment plans. Those with a terminal illness can no longer hope for a cure; however, they have expectations, wishes, and fears. Table 6.1 illustrates many of these that have been expressed over time by those who are dying.

Another tool for assessment and intervention is the 'Psychological needs' assessment (Table 6.2), referred to in previous chapters. This assessment helps patients and those involved understand the importance of these needs, and how they have been greatly altered; it initiates a process of compromise and setting goals for the attainment of these needs now and in the time that is still to come. Table 6.2 illustrates how this chart may be used with this population. For

Table 6.1   *Dying patients*

Expectations and wishes of a dying person

1. To be treated as a living human being (body, mind, and spirit) until death.
2. To maintain hope and have those who care for me remain hopeful.
3. To have my questions answered honestly, and not to be deceived.
4. To participate in decisions concerning my care, allowing me as much control over my life as possible.
5. To be able to express my experience of this living-dying interval of life.
6. To have others respect my choices concerning the way that I prefer to die and the disposition of my body.
7. To be alleviated from my pain as much as is humanly possible.
8. To provide support for my loved ones (if needed).
9. To share my spirituality with others and to receive spiritual nurturance from others.
10. To not die alone.

Fears of the dying patient

1. The fear of being alone.
2. The fear of the unknown.
3. The fear of regression.
4. The fear of losing self-identity and meaningful roles.

each need a different patient is used to show the variety of possible responses and goals. Designing goals for the future is done on a day-to-day or week-to-week basis. As mentioned in other chapters, the goals must be realistic, meaningful to the person (not the counsellor), and attainable.

The Cancer Counseling Center of Ohio works mainly with persons who have a life-threatening or chronic illness. Loss (of job, of money, of physical mobility, etc.) and possible death are constants in the treatment process. Zimpfer's (1992) holistic model includes perspectives that focus on the body, mind, spirit, and emotions. A spirit of harmony among these dimensions is sought, whether one strives to maintain a life amid losses, or whether one anticipates death. The model is based on the concept of wellness:

> wellness refers to positioning all the resources of the self so that they are neither competitive among themselves nor interfering. . . . In short the patient allows his or her body the full use of its capacities for healing by removing impediments and by optimizing its innate tendencies towards health. Healing in this instance implies not merely bodily recovery but also inner harmony and fullest use of personal potential. (1992: 205)

In the situation of life-threatening illness, anticipatory grief is compounded by uncertainty. At the Center, many clients have a disease

Table 6.2   *Psychological needs of dying patients*

Needs	Past	Present	Future
Love: Case example of a patient with a brain tumour who is aware, but unable to talk			
Who are the people whom I can trust and who love me and I can love in return? (family, friends)	Many friends Husband Children	Friends no longer stop by Unable to verbally communicate Husband can't tolerate changes in wife – gone all day and evening Paid professional caregivers	Transfers trust and caring to hospice staff
Belonging: Case example of a patient in end stages of breast cancer			
What do you belong to/feel comfortable with/feel part of and contribute to?	Family, friends, church, work, community	Treatments create negative side-effects – prevent active involvement in most of her past activities	Compromises and prioritizes – chooses 2–3 activities to remain minimally involved in Does phone support for others
Worth: Case example of a patient with a brain tumour, bedridden, and able to talk			
What do I do/or like about myself, that makes me feel good about myself?	Based on performance as a top salesman	Unable to see any self-worth outside of work roles Has packed away awards – can't tolerate the sight of them – memories too painful	Compromises – re-establishes a relationship with grandson – tells him stories of his days as 'top salesman'

continued overleaf

Table 6.2   *(Continued)*

Recognition: Case example of a patient bedridden with end-stages of prostate cancer

Who appreciates me and gives me recognition? What do I do that I feel is worthwhile and is important to me?	Previous role of 'head of household' and 'decision-maker'	Wife is now primary financial head of the household	Wife reinstates his power as 'head of the household' – sets up bed table as his desk to conduct the finances and make family decisions

Fun: Case example of a patient who is in the end stages of lung cancer

What do I do for fun – alone/with others? How much does it cost? How much of my fun is free?	Outdoor activities: hunting, fishing, camping	Bedridden – refuses hospital bed – sets up 'quarters' on family room couch Irritable – sullen – uncommunicative	Compromises – night before he dies – requests all of family to have a 'camping trip' in family room. Reminisces about past fun together

Freedom: Case example of a patient with lung cancer who is in transition to loss of mobility

What does freedom mean to me? Time, money, what I eat? Activities, what I say? Other choices	Had been an independent, travelling salesman – in total control of his time, money, decisions. Always had multiple choices	Stumbles – increased inability to move around. Family insists on a wheelchair. He refuses and continues to fall. Activities restricted to his living-room chair	Accepts wheelchair – sees it as a solution for more mobility and activities outside the living room and the house

which is potentially lethal, but not necessarily so. They face, as if this were not bad enough, the incursions and perhaps the worsening of bodily illness, difficult treatments and their often debilitating side-effects, and the loss of many aspects of their customary daily life; but they also face the possibility of dying. Treatments in these cases often must go beyond logic, information, and talk. Tools are routinely used which can access the internal states, the subliminal message systems, that lie beneath the surface of conscious aware-ness. It is our belief that where denial, doubt, and ambivalence prevail, clearer messages can often be obtained from the 'inner self'. Thus, mental imagery, searching for internal direction (i.e. intuition, what my 'heart' or my 'gut' tells me), and hypnosis are often used to clarify the issue of living or dying. Many concerns must be dealt with: the fundamental orientation to live or die; the will to persist or to give up; the desire to fight the illness using the standard medical treatments or to use alternative treatments or to let the body do its own work; and the reliance on God, on cosmic energy, or on some other higher power. Issues such as these are addressed as part of the fullness of the person, and to prevent their becoming impediments. They are involved in both the recovering and the dying process. Doubt about whether one is going to live or die, or even whether one wants to live or die, are tremendously complicating to the grief resolution process. Counselling involves evaluation of current life-style for modifications that are more consistent with physical abilities; attention to psychodynamics that allow for release of past resentments, guilt, and emotional pain; and resolving old inter-personal conflicts that may be interfering with inner peace.

In dealing with life-threatening illness, the practitioner treads a narrow line between counselling for living and counselling for dying. In our own experience we 'go with the flow' of the client, picking up on his or her basic direction. Occasionally a client will present what appears to be continual denial of the possibility of death, even in the face of worsening symptoms and physical decline and the ineffec-tiveness of medical treatments. Saying the unsayable may be appro-priate in this event (i.e. introducing the possibility of death to the client); it may unleash a cascade of fears and other emotions hitherto bound up in stoic silence. The counsellor must be cautious, however, that his or her own expectations or conclusions (about the inevitability of death) do not become prophecies to be imposed on the ill one. It is, after all, the client's life to live. As helpers we can nudge and prompt, but we cannot prod or push, in situations like this.

Counselling for the dying involves reinstatement of harmony of body, mind, spirit, and emotion. In the final stages of dying, the mind cognitively accepts the likelihood or inevitability of death; the emotions have resolved quarrels and guilts with other people living or dead, and have moved beyond anger at perhaps being cheated of a more productive life; the spirit has accepted whatever sense of immortality or nothingness, welcome or anonymity that may come after death; and the body prepares itself for dying, perhaps even by ceasing to fight with its own resources any longer.

Anticipating death, as it is seen in this chapter, is a property of both the dying person and the significant others (most often the family) around him or her. We have worked with families who were all present during the dying hours or days, who by turns held or caressed or breathed in unison with the ill person, who reminisced together, who cried and laughed together, and who in general turned what is often a solitary event into a loving community experience.

Issues for children and adolescents who have life-threatening, chronic, or terminal illnesses

Some young children and adolescents will not have the advantage of growing up without the burden of serious illnesses. For this population, ongoing tasks of development will still need to be addressed; however, these tasks will often be disregarded if medical care becomes dominant.

Fox (1991) discussed various issues and concerns with this population and suggested methods of intervention. She proposed that pre-school-age children would be concerned with four anticipatory grief issues: the cause of their illness, concerns regarding their bodies, anxieties over treatments, and a pervasive fear of dying.

Young children have self-focused ideas about their illness and often blame themselves for having done something wrong to cause it. Counsellors need to be aware of this and understand that thoughts such as these are most likely present, even if not verbalized. As children ask questions, reverse the queries and ask them why they believe that they are ill. Directly answering questions often results in missed opportunities to understand the fears and self-imposed blame behind questions that appear straightforward. Another major concern for this age group is the physical aspects of what is happening to their bodies. As they endure multiple treatments with various side effects, they often feel that their body belongs to the medical profession. Treatments often do not produce the desired effects, and relapses or negative side effects result. Most pre-school-age children do not understand how their bodies function; thus, these treatments and side effects often evoke anxieties that professionals are not aware of. A common fear for a child is to see big tubes of blood drawn from his or her small body, and to worry if there is enough blood left inside for them to live. They are unable to conceptualize the body's ability to continue to produce blood. An even greater concern is for those children who react too passively to treatment. It is psychologically healthier for children to fight treatment from time to time than to become overly conforming, with feelings of helplessness. Interventions must address the need for offering a child some control and decision in the treatment. Practitioners must assess the possibilities of choices they can give children. For example, they can give a treatment in the bed or on someone's lap where they might feel more secure. Inpatient programmes for children address many of these needs and provide secure environments for hospitalized children.

Lastly, this age group is very aware of the fact that they might die; and although they do not communicate this fear openly, they often express it in their actions. Spontaneous art work can offer important nonverbal, symbolic clues to the inner world and fears of acutely ill and/or dying children.

Many of the same issues apply to school-age children (from kindergarten to the age of 12 to 13). Techniques such as art and play are also used for this age group. A major difference is the fact that this group can communicate better, and they are capable of past and future cognitions. Future concerns are often verbalized or apparent in acting-out behaviours during the initial diagnosis or at times of relapse. This is often difficult to address directly because well-meaning adults fear reprimanding children who are seriously ill. Often this becomes a focus of interventions: acknowledging the distress that the child is experiencing, and at the same time setting needed behavioural boundaries. Relapses often mean additional hospitalization and disruption in their school and social environments. Since school-age children are mature enough to be aware of their future, adults need to be honest about potential future treatment and hospitalization. This age group needs a considerable amount of time to ask questions and to attempt to regain a sense of personal control.

Interventions must focus on more listening than talking. Counsellors must continue to ask themselves: 'What is this child really saying, and what is he or she internally working on?' Some helpers become overly concerned before meeting a child regarding what to say, what tools to use, etc. The primary intention should be to listen and to gain entry into the internal world of a child who has lost control of his or her own body. Often it might be more appropriate to meet with the parents first, especially if there is some uncertainty about how much the child understands about the illness. No matter what approach is chosen, the goals must include honesty, providing a safe environment, and listening. Interventions should include the provision of a network of supportive friends, family, and staff; flexible hospital policy; and creative strategies that provide opportunities for therapeutic play using different mediums (e.g. paint, sand, and water).

Adolescents who are seriously ill present a different challenge for professional caregivers. Simultaneously they are working on issues of development as well as fears of their non-being. Adolescents with life-threatening illnesses have a unique developmental confrontation. Tim, aged 17, was diagnosed with Hodgkin's disease following a car accident. He had always been active: athletics, the school band, and so on. He had shortness of breath after athletics practice, but thought nothing of it. It was the summer of his junior year and he was looking forward to all the promises of his senior year. The car accident was not life-threatening; however, complications that resulted led to the above diagnosis. The medical plan included surgery, then chemotherapy and radiation, with a prognosis of a cure before Christmas of his senior year. He just had to get through all the treatment and the lifestyle adjustments, and life would be the same again. Tim smiled during the sessions and told a good story: sure, he didn't like the treatment, and he certainly didn't like his early summer evening curfews. He had a girlfriend who had stayed by him during all this, and he wanted to have a good time with her. He felt fine three days after the chemotherapy, and believed he should be able to do what he wanted to do with his friends. His friends had been great. They continued to visit, and they talked about shaving their hair as a sign of support when Tim lost his from the treatment. So, what was wrong? What anxieties made it impossible for him to cope at times? With all this reassurance, positive prognosis, a semi-return to normality, and support, no one could assure him that he was not going to die. Exclusive focus on thoughts of the future and the normal dreams of adolescence were not a reality for Tim. He was confronted with the developmental tasks of planning for his future and contemplating his non-being at the same time. Control and choice are two important variables in treatment plans. Moreover, where an adolescent is in relation to specific developmental issues and simultaneously, where they are in the cycle of their illness (diagnosis, treatment, relapse) needs to be part of the ongoing assessments and interventions.

Krementz (1989) has raised awareness of adolescent issues from her interviews with teenagers with life-threatening illnesses. One female, aged 15, had been coping with lupus since the age of 8. She talked about the physical effects of this illness, and also the developmental concerns of an adolescent. She expressed a desire to be less dependent upon her mother in many areas that she lacked control in because of the illness. A major concern was her inability to take part in normal activities and her mother's overprotectiveness of her, resulting in an inability to go to new places and experience a fuller life.

Working with children and adolescents who have life-threatening, chronic, or terminal illnesses presents numerous challenges that are unique to their age and developmental level. Often the task of a developmental level (e.g. adolescent tasks) will take precedence (in the mind of the patient) over medical concerns and advice. Children who require extensive medical treatment also need to attend to their childhood needs for play and socialization, and development of trust, initiative, and autonomy. Professionals must be aware of these needs and ensure that there is the opportunity for children to develop and enjoy life as much as possible within their medical condition. They cannot be treated as fragile and incompetent, nor denied opportunities to experience life. On the other hand, medical interventions cannot be ignored, nor can the child or adolescent be allowed to be irresponsible because he/she is ill.

7

Special Issues

Every loss has special features, and for each individual experiencing a loss, there are unique issues. While this chapter cannot address the numerous issues or the variety of hardships that must be endured after every loss, it will focus on certain special losses wherein resolution of grief can be more difficult. Included will be trauma in general, murder, suicide, AIDS, and perinatal/neonatal loss.

Inherent in these types of loss is the concept of disenfranchised grief. Disenfranchised grief, as defined by Doka, is the 'grief that persons experience when they incur a loss that is not or can not be openly acknowledged, publicly mourned, or socially supported' (1989: 4). He has proposed three possible reasons for this occurrence: (1) the relationship is not recognized; (2) the loss is not recognized; (3) the griever is not recognized. This type of grief is often more intense because of situations surrounding the loss. Moreover, these situations frequently cut off sources of needed emotional support. AIDS is a good example of disenfranchised grief in which non-traditional relationships are often not recognized or socially sanctioned, nor is the griever recognized as a legitimate griever. Often early pregnancy loss is not recognized as a legitimate loss, and there are hidden issues of intense loss and grief to cope with for those family members and friends who survive a death by suicide or murder. In addition to the griever not being recognized as a legitimate griever, there are often characteristics about the griever that discount their status as legitimate grievers. Young children, the elderly, and the developmentally disabled are frequently ignored in their grief. Work with the developmentally disabled has increased our awareness about the variety of losses that this population has experienced without social support or recognition. This group is often viewed as not having the same psychological and human needs as the rest of the population.

Trauma

Many losses occur within what would be considered traumatic events. Trauma, however, is not just loss. It involves dealing with circumstances that have catastrophic components. Some type of violence occurs at the same time as the loss. Earthquakes, fires, and floods are examples of natural disasters that are considered traumatic. Initially individuals experiencing such disasters are involved with the major ordeal of surviving the event, and then immediately are forced to face the reality that loved ones may not have survived. Multiple losses may follow natural disasters: loss of homes and their contents, loss of personal control and security, loss of a past lifestyle, and so forth.

Trauma can also be experienced through violent acts such as murder, rape, war, hijackings, and varied forms of attack and destruction. The bombing of the federal building in Oklahoma City in the United States in the Spring of 1995 traumatized the survivors, the friends and families of the deceased, the local community, and the nation as a whole. For the friends, families, and the community losses were apparent and similar to what is experienced after natural disasters. However, there were other losses for these individuals and for the nation as a whole. Basic rights had been violated. No longer could people say that what had been perceived as a safe place to live and raise a family would ever again fulfil that role. No longer could they be assured that they lived in an environment where their rights could be protected by their government. Innocent people had been assaulted because a system was deemed unacceptable. As the nation watched the events that followed the bombing, many echoed symbolic losses: loss of security, loss of trust, and loss of belief in the power and ability of the system to ensure life, liberty, and the pursuit of happiness for its inhabitants. Personal belief systems were challenged as a result of this event, and losses reflected philosophical and spiritual perspectives, as well as the psychological, sociological, and physical. And for some who had been victims of other traumas, such as war, flashbacks and negative reactions emerged as a result of this wanton violent act.

Special considerations

Raphael (1992) discussed concepts and manifestations of trauma. The traumatized individual is often dealing with a double psychological burden: a post-traumatic stress reaction (PTSR) and a bereavement response. Both may occur concurrently, or the PTSR may override the loss. It will be important for the counsellor to assess which process should be responded to first. In any case, the trauma of the loss must always be dealt with; and if it has not been addressed prior to professional intervention, counselling must begin here. This initial acknowledgement may include a verbal and detailed repetition of the event, looking at pictures and objects, or a return to the scene of the crisis. Not to address trauma first opens the possibility that an individual will become 'locked in time' and not move past the event psychologically.

The emotional stress of trauma includes a sense of powerlessness, the horror of having witnessed suffering, identification with the victims (e.g. same age), overinvolvement in efforts to save individuals, and lastly, the experience of grief associated with the loss. Trauma leaves an imprint cognitively and visually, and reminders are usually present in the survivor's environment. Behavioural responses may include denial, disassociation, arousal, repression, and/or splitting.

Raphael (1992) further proposed some patterns that could occur over time with various risks for pathology. She stated that a post-traumatic reaction could evolve into a disorder (PTSD) and that pathological grief could develop if the issues involved with the crisis are overlooked or avoided. As previously mentioned, there are risks that individuals can become fixated to the trauma. There remains personal vulnerability well past the traumatic experience, and often there is a failure of needed support to help work through the multiple issues involved. As with other types of loss, once the event has occurred, initial support has been offered, and some time has passed, most people external to the loss do not perceive any additional problems or need for support. Moreover, just as every loss has secondary losses, trauma includes secondary or symbolic losses and secondary traumatic reactions, especially when it becomes drawn out in legal processes.

Interventions

1. Support individuals through shock, horror, and numbness. Deal with the needs as they are presented.
2. Review the circumstances of the event. Many try to avoid this because of the recall of the horror and the violence associated with it.
3. Intervene to help the client deal with the affect resulting from the event: fear, helplessness, shock, anxiety, anger, guilt. Address these affects in manageable amounts.
4. Assist the individual to gain mastery and control over the trauma through review, release of affective responses, and working through whatever needs to be addressed. People have to work through what they think they could have done differently. It is important to help clients reconstruct what has occurred.

Suicide

Suicide is an unspeakable loss. People in Western cultures find it difficult to listen to those bereaved after a suicide. The legacy of the persons left behind is shame, fear, guilt, rejection, anger, and distorted thinking, in addition to their sense of loss. Suicide puts psychological skeletons in the closets of survivors.

Special considerations

Suicide presents a triple threat. It is usually a sudden death that happens without any time to prepare for it. It means the loss of a significant person in the lives of many. And it is an action loaded with emotional content. Survivors may become preoccupied, thinking that perhaps they were to blame or that they could have done something to prevent the outcome. The presumption of guilt runs as a thread through the whole bereavement process.

Suicide leaves a stigma on individuals and on families as a whole. Families develop conspiracies of silence, and often fail to talk to each other about the event and issues underlying it. Family members take on different roles after a suicide. Some play the role of detective and want to track down clues. Others try to suppress the whole matter. The emotional impact on the family centres on denial (disguising the cause of the death), anger (focus on one cause or person as 'scapegoat'), and guilt (moral failure or self-blame). Survivors ask value questions of themselves and others. They seldom answer the whys satisfactorily, and often fear most what they understand the least. The impact upon the survivors leaves great emotional suffering. Day (1992), after the suicide of her husband, described this loss as 'the ultimate abandonment', with anger being her greatest emotion. The social impact is one of social awkwardness, as there are no explicit rules or guidelines after a suicide. Survivors often retreat into themselves and experience feelings of rejection and abandonment ('he or she chose to leave me'). These feelings in turn lead to a sense of hopelessness. At other times there are feelings of relief if the person had caused difficulties for some time and had emotionally drained those around him/her. This feeling is later replaced with guilt.

Interventions

1. When appropriate, follow the interventions suggested for dealing with trauma.
2. Address the major emotions (Humphrey et al., 1990):

   Shame is a predominant affect for suicide survivors, because suicide is a stigma within Western societies. Encourage clients to talk about the event openly. Help conduct a psychological autopsy. Review the events leading up to the death, but help them understand suicide as a long-term process and not just a singular event. Using the term 'completed' instead of 'committed' helps facilitate an understanding of suicide occurring over time, with the death as the completion.

Encourage families to talk about it together. Suicide often involves two or more survivors. Break a family's conspiracy of silence by encouraging family sessions. Counsellors should address the family as a system (see Chapter 4). If the counsellor is the only outlet for the client, he/she may get pulled in as part of the problem. The client will find talking to the counsellor safer and more comfortable, thus avoiding important family discussions.

Guilt is often manifested in self-punishing behaviours, such as overeating, the use of drugs, or alcohol. Help the client reality-test his or her guilt. Advise that most guilt is irrational. Ask clients: 'Exactly what could you have done differently? What did you do? What else did you do? Whom did you tell?' Questions such as these assist individuals in processing their guilt, testing the appropriateness of it, then reframing their understanding of the death.

Anger is frequently misdirected. Assist clients in understanding that their anger is directed at the deceased. Help them identify what they do not miss about their loved one. This facilitates the necessary process of building a balanced picture, and helps the release of anger to be properly directed.

Fear underlies the entire bereavement experience of the survivor. Assure clients that suicide is not hereditary. Educate clients about the signs of depression and suicide.

3. Use cognitive interventions to address distorted thoughts that often predominate. Help the client get accurate information before rumours about the death get started. Address cognitive distortions as they arise.

Murder

Unexpected, sudden death of a significant other in one's life through murder violates an individual's sense of security and control. Grief reactions are usually severe and intense. They are often exaggerated, with numerous complications. Support will be needed, at various levels, and for a longer period of time. Survivors of homicides often need additional coping mechanisms (Humphrey et al., 1990).

Special considerations

Redmond (1989) discussed several characteristics of issues underlying a homicide that must be understood and considered in assessment and interventions:

Cognitive dissonance refers to the inability of the mind to comprehend something that does not match its perception of reality as it had previously been known. The violent act of murder is difficult to comprehend and place within one's framework of personal reality and understanding. It goes beyond the normal coping mechanisms of shock, numbness, denial, and disbelief. It is often beyond human comprehension, and additional cognitive and affective mechanisms are required in order to adequately process the experience.

Revengeful impulses on the part of homicide survivors involve normal anger compounded by rage. Many fantasize acting out this rage, and it is important to validate this feeling as normal. One mother fantasized cutting off the head of her daughter's murderer with the lawnmower. Mowing the lawn facilitated an expression of this impulse and provided an emotional outlet for the intensity of her feelings.

Fear and vulnerability is an integral part of the bereavement experience. Families fear further harm to themselves, family members, and friends. The same mother could not stay alone in her home, and went to a neighbour's house at 5.30 a.m. when her husband had left for work. She feared that the friends of the murderer would return to harm her, as he had threatened this after he had been arrested.

Coping as a survivor of a murder involves a *conflict of values and belief systems*. As discussed in Chapters 1 and 2, loss and the experience of grief are influenced by a number of perspectives, including the philosophical and spiritual. The difference after a murder is that the influence of these two perspectives is more intense, with little positive influence being contributed from past losses. For example, if the spiritual perspective had previously contributed a positive influence that allowed individuals to cope more effectively with loss, in the case of murder it may not offer any support, and may exert a negative influence instead. Anger may be directed at God, as the bereaved experience a severe loss of faith and trust in a higher power.

In many communities, murder carries a *stigma*. Some blame the survivors or the victim, for somehow 'allowing it to happen'. Ascribing blame allows others to hide behind a false sense of security (i.e. 'This will never happen to me').

In addition to the grief, survivors also have to contend with *systems* that they have little knowledge or understanding about, such as law enforcement, the courts, and the media. The survivors become victims because of these intrusions. 'Secondary victimization' has been described by homicide survivors and often said to be more severe than the trauma of the murder itself. Secondary victimization corresponds to a number of the characteristics defined in the concepts of disenfranchised grief: the type of grief is more intense because of situations surrounding the loss, secondary victimization is not identified or understood as a loss, and an individual who is forced to cope with various systems in society after a murder is not recognized as bereaved. Often they are subtly accused as participants or contributors to the death, or even as perpetrators.

Interventions

1. Address issues of trauma as needed.
2. Offer a full range of supportive services over an extended time. This enables survivors to address pertinent issues as they arise, develop effective coping behaviours, and integrate the experience in order to rebuild their lives.
3. Educate clients regarding the various systems that they will have to deal with (e.g. terminology, policies and procedures).
4. Provide an environment that validates and encourages a full range of emotional expression in order to gain a sense of empowerment.
5. Use cognitive methods to address distorted thinking, guilt and self-blame. Encourage ongoing and honest communication among family members.

AIDS

Doka (1989) stated that there are relatively few other areas in the field of loss where the concept of disenfranchised grief is more powerfully demonstrated. He has outlined unique aspects of AIDS grief, giving the practitioner a basis for assessment and intervention:

1. There is a powerful social stigma associated with this illness and death. Individuals have reported an intense experience of alienation and rejection.
2. There is a lack of social sanctions, especially when the relationship was a homosexual one.
3. There is a concern and a fear on the part of survivors for their own physical health.
4. There is an inordinate need for secrecy on the part of families, coupled with shame and guilt.

Special considerations

Those with AIDS and families of victims are likely to be morally judged by society and deemed unworthy of inclusion in daily activities. Support is virtually nonexistent, and those involved are left on their own to cope with a long-term and devastating illness, death, and intense and far-reaching repercussions. Much of the stigma originates from the past reality that this was an illness that was almost exclusive to the gay community or to those involved in the drug culture (two segments of society already alienated and disenfranchised). Although awareness of the facts is rapidly changing, attitudes and needed support fall far behind. Lack of knowledge regarding transmission of AIDS is another factor that influences many to keep their distance. Examples of this have been observed in the alienation of school-age children who have family members with AIDS, or who have been diagnosed as HIV positive.

Other factors influencing alienation often come from within the victim's family of origin, especially if the illness was a result of an alternative lifestyle. Some families cannot accept these differences in each other, and often reject those members who have chosen a homosexual relationship. The patient is not socially sanctioned in society, nor is he or she sanctioned as a family member. Closing the patient out often results in the family becoming isolated from prior community involvements and potential support. They create part of their own alienation, and they move back and forth between blaming the patient and self-blame and guilt. Parents have difficulty in not being able to answer certain questions, and subsequently continue to ask each other, 'Where did we go wrong?' Shame and guilt predominate, and fear that their secret (a family member with AIDS) will become known is a driving influence. One example is a family who moved to another part of the country where no one knew them prior to the terminal stages of their son's illness and subsequent death. Even after the death they continued patterns of avoidance and secrecy, making it difficult to take advantage of professional services.

Lastly, for those who do belong to the gay community, in some cases, there has been a perceived sense of alienation from friends who they expected to offer support. Part of this is because this community has been overwhelmed with loss from AIDS, and may lack the emotional resources necessary for support over extended periods of time. Others have declared in counselling sessions that they have pulled back on their involvement as supporters because they are dealing with conflicted and ambivalent emotions towards friends who are infected, and towards the significant others who have been left to grieve alone. They have said that they need time to process these feelings and integrate the illness/dying experience of so many, and to reflect on how they have been affected.

Although the above considerations are part of other loss experiences, they appear to be more intense in this type of illness and death. AIDS, in many respects, can be termed the modern-day leprosy, carrying with it stigma, fears, alienation, and issues of disenfranchisement.

Interventions

AIDS calls for interventions both during the illness and after the death; however, the following will only address those bereaved following the death of a loved one.

1. Identify and address issues of grief that have not been socially recognized or sanctioned.
2. Validate the relationship and loss as legitimate and important to the bereaved.
3. Explore areas of guilt, anger, and ambivalence, or unfinished business with the deceased that may not be recognized or verbalized by the bereaved.
4. Explore concerns of health and future well-being on the part of the bereaved.
5. Assess current and future social supports, and address real or perceived alienation. Assess current family support.
6. Encourage memorialization, especially if the bereaved was denied participation in a funeral rite.
7. Support and become actively involved in helping the client regain a sense of personal control and power.
8. Identify and assist the client to address any issues related to AIDS that need clarification, correct information, education, or professional involvement.

Early loss of a child: miscarriage and perinatal deaths

Parental loss of a child, as discussed in Chapter 4, is one of the most difficult and intense losses to cope with. The age of the child will bring unique issues along with it; however, one of the most unrecognized losses within the broader category of parental loss is miscarriage, stillbirths, and other early deaths following childbirth. These losses have been called 'lonely', because often the mother has been left to grieve the death of her child alone. Often parents must say goodbye to their child before they even say hello. If the father has not bonded with the child during pregnancy, it is often difficult for him to grieve, or to understand what his wife is experiencing. For all, the grief process is more difficult because what is being grieved often is a dream. How one grieves and the specific issues to be addressed will relate strongly to how the parents had fantasized the child. A wished-for child may have represented various hopes and expectations. Many pregnancies are replacements for former losses; many have been planned to save the marriage or with the expectations of giving one's life meaning and purpose. The experience and resolution are more difficult, and much of the healing process takes place on a symbolic level.

Special considerations

In order to understand and intervene effectively, it is first necessary to understand the concept of attachment with regard to pregnancy. Kennell and Klaus (1976) have proposed nine steps that occur in this process:

1. Planning the pregnancy
2. Confirming the pregnancy
3. Accepting the pregnancy
4. Feeling foetal movement
5. Accepting the foetus as an individual
6. Giving birth
7. Hearing and seeing the infant
8. Touching and holding the infant
9. Caring for the infant

Note that the first five steps occur before the birth. Understanding that the greater part of the attachment process is completed before the birth helps bring into focus the nature of the human attachment, and the need to validate and support the difficult issues of grief and resolution.

Nichols (1986) discussed specific grief symptoms associated with this loss:

Physical: Emptiness, aching arms, slight sense of unreality, body tension, lack of strength, blurred vision, and palpitations.

Emotional: Sadness, anger, guilt, depression, death-related anxiety, pining for what 'might have been', sense of failure, and inability to accept reality.

Mental: Preoccupation with thoughts of the baby, hallucinations, fantasies or dreams about the baby; fear of going crazy; and confusion/ preoccupation of thoughts and memories of the deceased.

Social: Desire to be left alone; difficulty planning for the future; and social distance from, and problems communicating with one's mate.

Mothers often carry the burden of the grief alone and lack adequate support systems. There are no stories or memories to share about this child, and significant others have not had a relationship with this child. Pictures are often few, and taken by hospital

personnel after the infant's death. Memorabilia are usually a foot-
or hand-print and a small lock of hair. For the parents, these items
are treasures; but for well-meaning sources of support, they have
little meaning and are an inadequate basis for remembering
and memorializing, two important components of grief work and
resolution.

Some of the common characteristics of grieving mothers include
the fact that most women remember the specific details surrounding
the loss for many years. Many women have reported some distance
or discomfort with their doctors. They felt that the doctor was too
busy to answer additional questions as they arose months after the
death. Many report strained marital relationships. The major source
of this problem is that the husband has not had the opportunity to
develop a strong emotional attachment with the deceased infant.

Interventions

1. If possible, help the parents complete the last three steps of
    attachment by providing the opportunity to see the infant, hold
    the infant, and to care for the child as if he/she were alive. This
    would include dressing the baby, caressing him/her, rocking him/
    her, and selecting clothing for the funeral.
2. Facilitate the process of assisting parents to plan the funeral and
    meaningful rituals.
3. Encourage memorialization. Many give gifts at Christmas to
    those less fortunate, in the name of their deceased infants.
4. Encourage parents to look at whatever pictures or objects they
    have and tell the stories of their hopes, dreams, and expectations
    of this wished-for child.
5. Encourage journal writing. They can reflect upon and write
    about any aspects of the pregnancy, birth, and death that they
    can remember.
6. Address difficult feelings associated with this loss:

    Guilt: a constructive and positive way to handle guilt is to find
    out everything possible about what happened. Prompt clients to
    ask direct questions and ask for honest answers. Encourage them
    to risk asking if anything that they had done made a difference.
    Advise them that sometimes there are no answers.

    Fear: encourage parents to list their fears. Listing them allows
    individuals to look at them one by one, and not feel so over-
    whelmed. Many fear future pregnancies and losses. Sharing fears
    with another can help diminish them. Everyone will have a
    different perspective and this allows for re-evaluation and new
    integration and meaning.

Anger: anger is almost a universal grief reaction. Anger in this loss is more difficult because it often lacks a focus. The medical staff may become a focus of parental anger. As with other clients in grief, help these clients find healthy outlets. If their anger is justifiable, the counsellor is often put in the position of becoming an advocate for this individual within the medical system. Advocacy is an important component of the counselling profession. It includes getting information, connecting clients to resources, and representing clients as needed in various decisions and negotiations that might affect their welfare and future.

7. Encourage clients to re-evaluate their environment and what they are doing, or not doing. A bedroom decorated as a nursery in anticipation of the birth should not become a shrine.
8. Advise against a pregnancy in the near future that is an effort to replace the deceased child before the grief has been fully experienced.

Other losses

There are other unique, difficult, or horrendous losses that many are forced to cope with, resolve, and find reasons to reinvest in life again. There are losses that many are forced to live with that can make death appear to be the better alternative. These include floods and other natural disasters, fire, industrial injuries, chronic illnesses, job loss, rape, assault, robbery, random violence, forced relocation, and other circumstances in which loss and grief are key components. These examples have been intended to raise an awareness that different losses may appear similar yet they raise unique issues. This awareness is intended to remind the practitioner of the need to explore all areas of a client's loss, and build interventions to meet the idiosyncrasy of each case.

8

When Grief is not Resolved

The nature and symptoms of unresolved grief have been discussed and debated over the past several decades. Many who have contributed to general models of loss and bereavement have also laid foundations for the conceptualization of unresolved/abnormal grief. The focus of this book is on mental health services for uncomplicated grief, yet it is important to understand the limits of one's competence. The purpose of this chapter is to broaden an understanding of potential problem areas within the realm of unresolved grief, but not to deal in depth with them.

A familiar question that we are asked is, 'When is grief not normal?' A practitioner must know the boundaries of normality, since the manifestations of normal grief often appear to be abnormal. It is important to have relevant criteria for assessment and to understand the limits of interventions. Moreover, counsellors need to know when a client's issues are beyond their professional scope, and a referral is indicated. Despite disagreement in some areas, there is general agreement that unresolved grief which becomes diagnosable as a syndrome or as a mental or physical disorder can have social, psychological, and medical implications for the larger society, and warrants intensive professional intervention. Many who have had multiple admissions and confinements on psychiatric wards and to mental institutions have been diagnosed with multiple losses, never resolved, from childhood onwards.

Definitions

The *Diagnostic and statistical manual of mental disorders* (DSM-IV) (American Psychiatric Association, 1994) defines unresolved grief in terms of symptoms that can be identified as not being characteristic of a normal grief response. Moreover, these bereavement symptoms can be differentiated from symptoms of a major depression. The symptoms of unresolved grief include:

1. Guilt about things other than actions taken or not taken by the survivor at the time of death. 2. Thoughts of death other than the survivor feeling that he or she would be better off dead or should have died with the deceased person. 3. Morbid preoccupation with

worthlessness. 4. Marked psychomotor retardation. 5. Prolonged and marked functional impairment. 6. Hallucinatory experiences other than thinking that he or she hears the voice of, or transiently sees the image of, the deceased person. (1994: 684)

Horowitz, Wilner, Marmar, and Krupnick (1980) used the terms pathological grief and mourning to describe problems in grief resolution:

Pathological grief is the intensification of grief to the level where the person is overwhelmed, resorts to maladaptive behavior, or remains interminably in the state of grief without progression of the mourning process toward completion. Pathological mourning involves processes that do not move progressively toward assimilation or accommodation but, instead, lead to stereotyped repetitions or extensive interruptions of healing. (1980: 1157)

Brayer (1977) used the term 'pathological grief' and defined it in relation to Freud's theory of mourning: a manifestation (on the part of the bereaved) of self-reproach and self-reviling that lead to delusional expectations of punishment.

Parkes and Weiss (1983) defined unresolved grief as abnormal, and stated that this occurs when recovery fails to take place. Recovery was then defined as the ability to replan one's life and to achieve an independent level of functioning.

Stephenson (1985) defined unresolved grief as 'exceptional grief'. He stated that grief can be labelled exceptional when there has been a 'lack of recognition of a significant loss, an extreme reaction far in excess of normative cultural expectations, and a lack of movement through the grief process' (1985: 151).

Demi and Miles (1987) delineated 31 manifestations of normal grief, but only define them as pathological when any one of the manifestations occurs five years post-bereavement.

Rando (1993) defined this phenomenon of pathological, abnormal, or unresolved grief as complicated mourning. Her definition allows for personal involvement and choice. This term does not pathologize grief, as do other definitions.

Referring to the bereavement models of the theorists in Chapter 1, unresolved grief is a consideration of each one, with similarities and variations between the conceptualizations.

Reference to theoretical models introduced in Chapter 1

Freud's conceptualization of loss, grief, and resolution focused on the acknowledgement and acceptance by the ego that the object had been lost, that the energy that had been used to maintain the attachment had been withdrawn, and that energy to make new attachments had been mobilized. He stated that grief is hard work and takes a considerable amount of time; however, unresolved grief is a different issue. He did not base his theory of unresolved or pathological grief on the amount of time it took to complete the process; instead, in *Mourning and melancholia* (1957), he proposed that ambivalence in a relationship can be the root cause of unresolved grief and mourning. 'Melancholia' was a term that Freud used for psychiatric depression, and he stated that this condition may be caused by the real or symbolic loss of a person. According to his theory, the lost person is incorporated in some manner within the bereaved individual. Once this has been accomplished, the bereaved can then persecute and punish the lost figure for having abandoned him or her. The lost person is very much alive in the unconscious and the bereaved does not withdraw energy from what has been lost to make new attachments. This theory is not accepted by practitioners today, as further research has provided better explanations of pathological guilt after ambivalent relationships.

Lindemann (1944) was one of the first to apply his concepts to assessment and intervention. From his study of the survivors of the Coconut Grove fire in Boston, he proposed that there can be distorted manifestations of the normal expressions of grief. During his clinical interventions he observed a tendency on the part of his clients to resist the pain of grief and the bereavement process. This denial or avoidance seemed to be the most significant contributor to distorted manifestations of grief and potential problems in resolution. There is a period of avoidance that is psychologically therapeutic. To feel numb or to initially deny that a loss has occurred allows needed time for the mind to adjust to the full impact of the loss event. According to Fulton, implicit in Lindemann's work is the

> assumption that 'normal' people will, under 'normal' circumstances, experience a 'normal' grief reaction and ultimately return to a 'normal' state of well-being. Researchers have observed that when this pattern is upset in any way, such as the lack of conclusive or persuasive evidence that a death has occurred, or when an initial denial reaction is not overcome, maladaptive responses to loss may occur. (1977: 7)

The major criticism of Lindemann's work is that he gave no indication of the frequency of these distortions over a time period, and that he led practitioners to believe that interventions could be used to resolve these distortions in four to six weeks (Parkes & Weiss, 1983). Research since his study has indicated that resolution involves a more arduous and cyclical process, and that it is difficult to predetermine the number of weeks needed. Lindemann, despite some of the shortcomings in his study, was one of the first to describe specific symptoms that were characteristic of complicated grief. In addition to denial, he proposed that overactivity without a sense of loss, acquisition of the symptoms of the deceased or development of some other medical disease, severe alterations in relationships with family and friends, schizophreniform behaviour, abnormal hostility toward specific persons, self-destructive behaviour, and agitated depression were all indicative of potential distortions and maladaptive adjustment after loss.

Kubler-Ross, in *Death: The final stage of growth* (1975), addressed philosophical, spiritual, and sociological/cultural perspectives that influence various cultures' difficulties with the death and dying experience. She stated that cultures that have prescribed rituals for bereavement resolve loss and grief more readily. Resolution is more likely to be achieved with a sense of transpersonal growth when there are prescribed ways of experiencing the process, and when there is validation and permission to grieve within a close supportive community. In these types of cultures loss, especially death, is integrated into their understanding of life. Unresolved grief is often the product of cultures that deny or avoid death.

Bowlby's (1969, 1973, 1980) studies provided an understanding of human attachment and a framework for understanding the potential for complicated grief when these attachments are threatened or broken. Bowlby made it clear that the early loss of a significant attachment figure is not necessarily the root cause of future pathology; however, depending upon a number of different factors, early loss can predispose an individual to adult problems. One reason is that the normal process of searching for what has been lost is often hastened to the point of being negated. Time may not be taken to go through this painful process of searching, with subsequent anger when the lost person cannot be found or retrieved. Children often have the tendency to resist this search, and to prematurely state that the loss has been accepted. What happens psychologically is that the lost object (not searched for and eventually relinquished) is kept alive in the unconscious. Thus the child without awareness keeps the search alive, and this influences future losses and personality development. Fixation, repression, and splitting of the ego are common defence mechanisms involved, with pathological mourning and future psychiatric illnesses occurring as typical outcomes of this type of early childhood experience with loss. Another contributing factor is the type of relationship and the personality characteristics of the bereaved. As noted by other theorists, ambivalent relationships and characteristics such as dependency and compulsive caregiving often are indicators of problems with resolution after loss.

Bowlby (1980) also proposed that how one has experienced early relationships and the roles of early attachment figures can greatly influence bereavement. What he has called 'cognitive biases' are important determinants of reactions to future losses and attachments. Unhealthy and unfulfilling early attachments influence the loss experience, as the bereaved views the present based on cognitions and beliefs developed early in life.

Worden (1991) listed five factors regarding failure to grieve: relational (e.g. ambivalent or narcissistic relationships); circumstantial (e.g. uncertainties regarding death or multiple losses); historical (e.g. past complicated losses such as early loss of parent); personality (e.g. how one copes, or how well one is integrated); and social (e.g. socially unspeakable death or lack of support systems). He further discussed types of complicated grief and showed the relationship of each complication to his 'tasks of grief' work. He suggested that assessment identify which tasks have not been completed, and that intervention begin at this point of immobility before attempting to continue through the normal tasks of grief counselling. One example would be delayed or inhibited grief, in which the bereaved has not been able to get in touch with or express the emotions involved. Although there may be various reasons for this difficulty, Worden suggests that the counsellor view the client as having a problem expressing the emotion of grief, and proceed to focus assessment and intervention on this task. The counsellor would explore the nature of the relationship and the details of the death. Focusing on helping the client experience the pain is necessary for eventual healing. Other examples are those who have had highly conflicted or ambivalent relationships, and hesitate to discuss negative aspects. These situations and others can cause problems in resolution and promote delayed or inhibited grief. 'Grief therapy' is a term he uses to describe the idea that there is an area of complication in the individual's experience that needs to be addressed initially and resolved before the normal task work can be completed.

Rando, in *Treatment of complicated mourning* (1993), acknowledged and incorporated theories and terms used over the last few decades into her conceptualizations of complicated mourning. She states that '*complicated mourning* means that given the amount of time since the death, there is some compromise, distortion, or failure of one or more of the six 'R' processes' (1993: 149). Her belief is that in all forms of complicated mourning there is an attempt to either 'deny, repress, or avoid aspects of the loss, its pain, and the full realization of its implications for the mourner; or to hold onto and avoid relinquishing the lost loved one' (ibid.). Rando then further delineated two levels of potential responses when the process becomes complicated: symptoms and syndromes. Symptoms are indicators that there are definite problems in the process of bereavement; however, they do not meet the criteria for diagnosable disorders or syndromes as specified in the DSM-IV. Symptoms can be severe and usually appear in the psychological, behavioural, social, and physical areas of functioning. They must be assessed and understood in relation to an individual's unique grief experience. Interventions are needed; but care must be taken not to quickly diagnose them as a syndrome or a mental or physical disorder.

Rando (1993: 156) organizes syndromes under three headings:

Problems in Expression
   Absent mourning
   Delayed mourning
   Inhibited mourning

Skewed Aspects
   Distorted mourning
   Conflicted mourning
   Unanticipated mourning

Problems with Closure
   Chronic mourning.

Diagnosis of a syndrome follows the definitions given in the DSM-IV. Under each of these syndromes, she relates a problem area in one of the 'R' processes of mourning. For example, delayed mourning would be represented by an inability to react to the separation, which is the second 'R' process. As with Worden's concept of 'tasks' (1991), Rando believes that it is necessary to locate the difficulty or impasse in one of the Six 'R' processes, identify the complications and work that process through, before moving on to the next process. Impasses and interferences may occur more than once and at any point. None of the processes can be avoided or severely compromised if healthy resolution is to occur. Details of Rando's work with complicated mourning are available in her writings (1993).

Types of syndrome

Absence, inhibition, or delay of bereavement
Definitions and examples will be given for the types of distorted manifestations, using the works of a number of theorists.

Raphael (1983) stated that absence, inhibition, or delay of bereavement have similar characteristics when considered on a continuum of avoidance of the pain of loss. 'True absent mourning is rare because it requires that the mourner either maintain complete denial of the death or remain in a total state of shock – two quite difficult feats' (Rando, 1993: 155). Usually what is observed is extremely inhibited grief. Delayed grief is grief which is not manifested at the time of loss. When it emerges, sometimes years later, it is as fresh and intense as if the loss had just occurred. An example of this is when a loss, such as a death, occurs in the life of a child and well-meaning adults attempt to protect the child from pain and never discuss the death. Some time later, an unrelated event can trigger the memory of the death, and the grief emerges as if the loss is presently happening. Inhibited mourning has some similarities to delayed grief. However, unique to inhibited mourning is the avoidance of particular issues associated with the loss, and selective attention to others.

In addition to Raphael's work, significant contributions have been made by Deutsch (1937) and Bowlby (1980), who agree that these manifestations of inappropriate mourning are often a result of negative and highly ambivalent relationships. A typical example is the adult child idealizing the abusive parent upon his or her death because the painful issues of abuse cannot be acknowledged. Attention must be paid to both the positive and negative aspects of a relationship in order to integrate the full meaning of the relationship in healthy and realistic memory. Worden (1991) further discusses the possibilities of inhibited grief being manifested in physical and psychiatric symptoms. He terms this 'masked grief'; the physical signs (e.g. chest pains) or the psychiatric symptoms (e.g. panic attacks) may be real and diagnosable, but they cover up the reality of the avoided grief.

Distorted and conflicted mourning

Distorted and conflicted mourning have similarities. Conflicted mourning is highlighted by ambivalence in a relationship. Distorted grief also involves ambivalence; what differentiates the two is the intensity of specific emotions in the latter. Intense manifestations of guilt and anger are the primary grief responses in distorted grief. Research from Parkes and Weiss (1983) and Rando (1993) offer insight into these mourning responses. All human relationships have ambivalence (love–hate features). Bereaved individuals often have to deal with feelings of guilt after a death because they loved the person who died, but also disliked him or her at times. In conflicted grief the degree or intensity of ambivalence is much stronger and more difficult to resolve.

The death of a child is an example when both conflicted and distorted grief can occur. Parents invest a great degree of themselves in their children. Children represent the best and the worst features of the parents. These relationships are ripe for high degrees of ambivalence. Most parents have at least some negative thoughts and feelings about their children, and it is this reality of the normal parental relationship that can cause difficulty in grief resolution. In instances where children suffer untimely deaths, distorted and intense expressions of guilt and/or anger are often the main features of parental grief. Before normal grief work can be addressed, these emotions need attention.

An example of a loss that manifested both distorted and conflicted grief was the murder of an adolescent female by her boyfriend on the porch of her home while her parents watched. This death was an assault and an outrage in every respect. For almost two years it involved every segment of the community, the legal system, and a network of counselling and medical professionals. Aspects of distorted grief were the first dimensions that had to be addressed. Nine months were needed just to address the extreme feelings and manifestations of anger. As noted above, the hallmark of distorted grief is anger or guilt that becomes extreme and goes beyond the normal response. Intentional murder of one's child highly pre-disposes parents to distorted manifestations of grief. Following the conviction of the perpetrator, the anger was somewhat dissipated; however, grief manifestations moved immediately to distorted feelings of guilt. The murder had happened quickly, and with little warning; yet, as parents, they tormented themselves with questions of why they could not have protected their daughter on their own property. The guilt was never resolved, and the anger continued to surface each time parole was considered for the convicted murderer. In addition to distorted manifestations, conflicted guilt was also part of the experience. As discussed, ambivalence in a relationship is a hallmark feature of conflicted grief. This was a highly ambivalent relationship. Developmentally their daughter was involved in a period of normal rebellion, and there were many volatile disagree-ments that had never been resolved. One of the major sources of tension had been her relationship with the boy who murdered her. For two years her parents had fought to keep her away from him, as his reputation for 'trouble' was well known. She had defied her parents on many occasions and met with him behind their backs. When she finally decided she did not want to be associated with him any more, he could not tolerate the rejection and killed her. From this example, it is possible to understand the difficulties certain persons may have resolving grief or having a normal experience with it. For some the distortions can be addressed and resolved, and a normal process of bereavement facilitated; yet for others, the distortions continue to emerge for an indefinite period of time, hindering healthy resolution and reinvestment in meaningful living.

Unanticipated mourning

Unanticipated mourning predisposes individuals to difficulties because they have had no opportunity to prepare mentally or psychologically for the loss; thus their adaptive defences have not been mobilized. Examples include losses such as sudden deaths and natural disasters – assaults that affect every perspective discussed in Chapter 1. Many affirm the effects of the assault and devastation but do not understand the psychological demands thrust upon them by these events. Often disasters have forced individuals to question the meaning and fairness of life, and to assimilate and accommodate to new environments or lifestyles that they had not been prepared for. The nature of the crisis can be of such a magnitude that it takes some time beyond the event to process and assimilate the full extent of the destruction that has occurred. And often, the additional losses that emerge as a result create ongoing demands for psychological coping and readjustment. Terrorist bombings have created global awareness of the impact and far-reaching psychological effects of trauma and human destruction.

Chronic mourning

Chronic mourning is another category of potential concern for healthy grief resolution. This type of grief never seems to cease, as, for example, the client who continues to display signs of acute grief years beyond the loss. Counsellors who have assessed this syndrome are struck by the intensity of the grief, and state that it appeared to be so acute and fresh that they thought the loss had just occurred. Moreover, there has never been a hiatus in the emotions. That is, there was never a time in which the bereaved experienced some relief from pain or some return to equilibrium. Bowlby (1980), Parkes and Weiss (1983), Raphael (1983), Rynearson (1990), and Rando (1993) have offered valuable contributions to this concept.

Reasons for problems with grief resolution

Numerous reasons have been proposed as to why grief becomes complicated or unresolved. In addition to the awareness that past unresolved losses and pre-morbid tendencies in personality and functioning can affect resolution, issues can also stem from society and types of loss. Society often dictates the specific rituals for mourning and prescribes a timetable for their completion. Often the funeral is the only recognized and accepted ritual. After the funeral, the bereaved feel abandoned in their grief because the support systems vanish and they are left on their own to comply with an expected timetable. Society's push for a quick resolution often sets the stage for complications and difficulties in healing. Moreover, certain deaths and losses have the potential to activate complications and unresolvable issues. Suicide, homicide, AIDS, the death of a child, and various types of loss that receive no social validation are examples that provide a basis for unresolved grief or complications in the normal grief process, as discussed in Chapter 7.

Intervention

When clients present issues that reflect unresolved areas of grief, counsellors must make a decision regarding their expertise and scope of practice. A referral at this point of assessment might be the most appropriate decision. However, it is very likely that most counsellors will have clients who come for one reason, and later on in sessions the counsellors realize that unresolved losses from the clients' past are contributing to present difficulties. Loss is an integral part of life, and will, in some way, contribute to most issues presented in counselling. We are not suggesting that the mental health prac- titioner refer every case of complicated grief. We are suggesting that mental health practitioners have an understanding and awareness of symptoms and syndromes so that they will be assessing and ruling them out. Most complications can be handled, especially under supervision. One reason to have this knowledge is to avoid the neophyte's error of quickly addressing the presenting loss at face value, without taking into consideration any complicating factors that might be underneath and eventually hinder resolution. We have learned that it is not possible to address the current loss if past, unresolved issues have emerged. Moreover, experience in this field has verified our view that many who present themselves in counselling have issues of loss that go beyond the present situation. Many have past losses representing repressed or unfinished business that needs to be addressed, often before the current loss can be processed. If these issues go beyond the counsellor's skill or available time, a referral may be in order.

Case example: Bob – loss and grief masked in symptoms of PTSD and Vietnam

The following case example is of a client who had been treated for PTSD in various settings for the past 20 years.

'I now remember certain things about my childhood. I was five and playing with my marbles on my bed. They had been a gift from my uncle who had come to visit that day. All of a sudden Dad grabbed Matt off the bed and ran from the house. Now I remember the scene. I know that he died because he swallowed one of the marbles. I realize that I have lived with shame and guilt all these years.' (45-year-old Vietnam veteran)

Presenting issues for counselling were centred around symptoms of PTSD, violent headaches, flashbacks from the war, survival guilt, unrelenting anniversary reactions, and periods of deep depression. Bob had spent a short time in a veterans' hospital about seven years earlier, with minimal benefit from the interventions offered. He had recently been hospitalized for depression and became a patient of a local psychiatrist who referred him for counselling, but continued to prescribe his medications. In addition to the multiple medicines prescribed by the psychiatrist, a local family doctor was administering morphine shots on a weekly basis for his headaches.

For two years, sessions focused on the above symptoms and recurring episodes of PTSD and depression. On one occasion, he related that a man had called him claiming to be a cousin whom he had not seen since the age of five. Bob said he was sceptical and had refused to continue the conversation. Trust was a difficult issue for Bob. After this statement, it became apparent that Bob was not mentally present. He had done this before when flashbacks occurred, or when he decided it was too painful to continue talking. The routine had come to be to ask him where he was mentally. Usually he would reply that the walls had just gone up, and this would be the signal to back off. However, this time he continued and said he was on a bed playing with his marbles. His baby brother was there with him. All of a sudden his father grabbed the baby and ran. The baby died; subsequently, Dad abandoned the family, resulting in Mum's decision to take Bob and his sister to Ohio to live with his grandmother. His grandmother raised him, as his mother was not emotionally healthy. Until this time, he had never allowed this reality into conscious awareness. He now recognized that the baby had swallowed one of the marbles. In his young mind he had imagined that it had been his fault. The guilt was understandable and the confusion became apparent: the gift had been transformed into an object of shame and guilt that influenced daily life and carried a powerful message of negativity into the present. Vietnam was an event that many survived with minimal scars; however, for those who came from childhood backgrounds such as Bob's, Vietnam had more deleterious and long-lasting effects. Over the next decades Bob came to mistrust gifts and good feelings, as they seemed to represent pain and negativity.

It was a few weeks after this that Bob experienced a flashback that had never been clearly defined, but one that connected the war experience with his childhood experience: He was in the streambed. Eleven men had been assigned to this combat mission. The attack came. His captain abandoned them; several buddies were killed instantly. (His father had also abandoned him after his baby brother died and his wife had left him after he had been in Vietnam for a year.) He believed that he was the only one left in the streambed, about to die. He crawled under a pile of dead bodies to hide. Some days later another American unit found him. Only three of the 11 survived. The captain was never seen again. Two days later Vietnam was evacuated. He returned to the States, but not as a hero. He was a reject and felt abandoned by his own country. For many years he coped by using alcohol. He then married his present wife, and his long search for who he was and his journey to mental health began.

Issues of loss and grief from the war, the end of his first marriage, and the recent death of his grandmother were obvious issues of loss to address. The deeper, hidden losses of childhood – the death of his brother, the abandonment by his father, a dysfunctional mother, and multiple intangible losses – were buried. Eventually the focus of intervention shifted. PTSD and depression were symptoms masking deeper issues. Strategies switched to interventions based on theories of loss and grief, which address core issues of guilt and shame that were rooted in early childhood. Today Bob understands the connectedness of his past to his present. He continues to gain awareness of issues that have been repressed. From this awareness, he has also grieved past losses and has relinquished their tenacious hold. Emotionally he has been freed to explore fuller dimensions of himself and begin the journey toward self-actualization.

Bob could not begin a normal grief process until he had addressed the issues that were preventing the completion of this process. Issues such as these are often at the root of unresolved grief and may be present in many counselling sessions. Within the professional literature there are a number of terms defining unresolved grief. Although these terms are often synonymous with patterns of emotional disorder, it is questionable if there is ever a pure manifestation of a specific syndrome. Rather, it appears that within specific cases of unresolved grief, there are manifestations of components of various syndromes. Bob's situation exemplifies this. The extreme guilt that dictated his present life mirrored concepts of distorted grief. Distorted mourning is manifested in either extreme guilt or extreme anger (Raphael, 1983). Although Bob had periods of uncontrollable anger, guilt seemed to predominate, with strong roots in early childhood. For various reasons, Bob's grief was also delayed, laying the foundation for complications. There was not just one loss event, but multiple losses over decades that were never addressed, grieved, or resolved.

It is probable that counsellors in any part of the world today will have multiple issues of grief to address with their clients. It is predicted that there will be significantly more clients predisposed to complications, pathology, or inability to resolve grief. Increase in violence and more conflicted social relationships are only two indicators of future concerns. Counsellors need to be educated and trained at least to be aware of these additional issues, to handle what they are capable of, and to refer when appropriate.

9

Outreach in the Community

It is not enough for the counsellor to facilitate the grief process in isolation, nor is it reasonable to expect that potential clients will understand or even recognize as available the benefits of grief counselling. An important adjunct to face-to-face counselling is outreach into the community.

Readers of this book may add their own interpretations and viewpoints on needed outreach services within their communities. The concept of outreach includes education. In times of loss, there is confusion and uncertainty regarding behaviours that are helpful or not helpful. Education is the basic tool of knowledge, which provides potential power to take action. It complements the counselling process. If one accepts that loss is an integral part of life from birth to death, then education in various types of loss, potential impacts, and methods of coping is a valuable resource to make available within the community for groups of children or adults. This chapter addresses community outreach and training programmes. Examples will be given that highlight some of the groups that may request assistance for a variety of reasons: schools, churches, nursing home staff, and the corporate world.

Schools

Work in schools has had three areas of focus: education, crisis intervention, and postvention (follow-up). Education includes the following: teacher in-service training, education in the classroom, and parent education.

Education
Teacher in-service training has ranged from general topics of understanding loss in general (Chapter 1) to specific information regarding the unique issues of children's and adolescents' grief and interventions, to effective methods of handling crises within the school setting. Well known are the increasing number of schools in which chaos follows student suicides, teachers' deaths, bus accidents, and other traumatic events that involve the staff and student body. In-service training helps prepare educators for future crises.

In addition, students seem to be facing burdens beyond those associated with normal growth and development. A number of children experience loss from an early age, and many of these significant losses are not death-related. Educators have become aware that these students have difficulty learning because the losses have created emotional burdens that interfere with the cognitive abilities required for learning and retention. Many students come from divorced families, emotionally abusive environments, and/or have parents with chronic physical or emotional illnesses. It is not possible to ignore these issues and to teach effectively. These students resist learning and often distract others, disrupting attempts at both teaching and learning. Classroom teachers are not being asked to take on the role of counsellor; rather, they are being educated to raise their awareness of issues underlying problem students and ways to identify such students. They are also made aware of the fact that children grieve episodically over the span of their development, relying on repression and denial as coping mechanisms to keep their grief 'undercover'. It is not unusual for a student who experienced a significant loss in the primary grades to have grief work to do in later years. Many students who have been labelled 'bad' are bereaved individuals in need of intervention. It would be helpful for educators from the primary years to inform the next teachers and counsellors of significant events in the earlier years of students. Understanding the far-reaching effects of various losses provides a basis for intervention before problems become irreversible.

Teacher in-service training also validates the present reality of educators who are often overburdened by multiple demands in addition to instruction. In-service training addresses the fact that teachers also have their own issues of loss and grief that they bring into the classroom. They are encouraged to personally identify their issues and take care of their own needs to avoid burnout and professional impairment.

Education in the classroom (e.g. psychology, health, family life classes) always includes basic information about loss and grief, as presented in Chapter 1. When working with different age groups, it is important to make the discussion age-appropriate, and to adjust the concepts and vocabulary to the students' cognitive level of understanding. Presentations should involve student interaction. In the secondary-school levels, the 'history of loss' (Tables 9.1 and 9.2) is used as an exercise to promote awareness of possible losses that students may already have experienced. Although such a programme is designed to educate, the experiential component can provide the catalyst for students to seek professional help. They are reminded that often they can be unaware of the impact losses have

Table 9.1 *History of loss (case examples of adolescents)*

Loss	Age	Experience Feelings and behaviour	Unanswered questions	What changed? (money, residence)
Case 1				
Alcoholic parent	8	Lonely, scared	Why it started	No one happy
Divorce	9	Weird feelings – never knew what it was like	None – happened because my father drank	Everything – nothing has ever been the same – nothing has been good
Dog died	9	Sad	None – car hit him	No more pets – lost a good friend
Moving	9	Felt weird	None	Everything – friends, bedroom – everything
Abused	10	Hurt inside	Why did I get abused? Was it my fault?	I don't feel the same about myself any more
Aunt died	15	Sad, unhappy	Why did she die?	Not much – but was first to die in my family
Grandfather died	15	Real sad, didn't talk	Why did he have to die?	Lost my real father

continued overleaf

Table 9.1   (*Continued*)

Loss	Age	Experience Feelings and behaviour	Unanswered questions	What changed? (money, residence)
Case 2				
Dad died	7	I wouldn't even go to the funeral because I couldn't believe my father had left me	Why couldn't I just tell him I loved him one more time before he left me	*Everything*
Brother died	16	I felt that I had been lied to, or didn't anyone want to tell me about him. I was angry. All the time when he was living I only knew him as a friend and nothing else	Why did I only learn that he was my brother right before the funeral?	I can't trust anyone
Aunt died	17	I loved her. She was always so kind to me and I felt that God shouldn't have taken her away yet because I wasn't finished sharing with her	Why couldn't I just have been able to take her to her doctor's appointment like she wanted me to? But I was sick	I can't stop all these feelings

Reprinted with permission, Grief Center, Inc., North Canton, Ohio

Table 9.2 *History of loss (alternative form)*

Loss	Age	Experience (feelings/behaviours)
Divorce	12	Felt scared and confused. Was upset, worried a lot, asked questions.
	17	Father got remarried. Father is further away now, don't see him very much.
	18	I still feel a great deal of loss. I feel very lonely, like something very important to me is missing. Last evening I cried myself to sleep. I realized (wished) that I had someone who would act like a father towards me. I remembered all the good times my father and I had. We used to do a lot of things together, and all of a sudden it stopped. I no longer had a dad – someone (male) I could talk to and someone to listen. Sure, I have my mother, but it's not the same. There are organizations like Big Brother/Big Sister. I wish there was something that would offer a father. I think the presentation helped me bring this out and to tell (write) someone about it, instead of keeping it inside of me. This may seem stupid to whoever reads this, but this is how I feel.

Reprinted with permission, Grief Center, Inc., North Canton, Ohio

had on their lives. This exercise might not only raise awareness; it might also trigger painful emotions. Students are then encouraged to share this exercise with a teacher or school counsellor. When this programme is done in the classroom, the teacher is always present, monitoring reactions and intervening when necessary. In some classes, where there is a level of trust, this exercise is often shared as a group activity. Most students will put their names on the sheet and hand it in. Students, in one way or another, have used this experience to get the help they need. One student wrote a lengthy history and ended with: 'This may sound foolish to whoever reads this; but this is how I feel about everything that has happened to me. No one has ever cared to ask me about these things.' These educational sessions also include discussions about coping and support systems. The classroom teacher or school counsellor usually makes the request for an educational programme on loss and grief. Often this request is made because the teacher or counsellor is aware of students who have suffered losses.

Education for parents is frequently offered at monthly meetings of school/parent board meetings or after a loss or crisis has occurred within the school community. The basic themes of these presentations, whether or not they are at times of crisis, are to acknowledge the grief issues, to understand the process and the multiple perspectives involved, to validate their children's grief and to be available for long-term support. Parents are encouraged to be honest in their communications regarding what has occurred, to give age-appropriate information, and to be aware that the loss will have to be re-examined across the developmental span. New questions, requiring more detail, will be asked as children develop cognitively. Many parents believe that if a child is given information once, this is sufficient. In addition, they believe that they must protect their children from pain. Education broadens parents' understanding of the pervasive qualities of loss and grief from birth to death. To deny children the opportunity to experience inevitable times of loss and grief is to do them a disservice. They will have a distorted view of reality and lack effective coping skills that will be needed at some time during their lives.

One example of a parents' meeting was a lengthy evening session following the murder of a student. Parents first had to be educated regarding the nature and the process of loss and grief; however, even more importantly they needed to come together and share their own grief and horror, ask questions concerning the future welfare of their children, and receive reassurance that the school administration would offer needed support and counselling for the students who had been closely involved with the murdered student. Accurate information about the event itself and the bereavement process, the importance of support systems, and information about effective coping strategies were all important at this time because none of the parents had been involved in such a crisis; nor had any of them been educated in issues of loss and bereavement. Like other well-meaning adults, they had pieces of information, much of which was not accurate; and they were trying to rush their children through this crisis and impose upon them their own solutions for coping.

Crisis intervention

A major programme offered by the Grief Support and Education Center in Ohio for the past number of years has been to train crisis teams from every school district within the county. In addition to this basic training, the Center offers day-long workshops with continuing education units for more in-depth study of children and adolescents experiencing grief, follow-up strategies after crisis, and crisis team management.

Another outreach service within the school setting has been direct involvement when a crisis occurs. The Center provides counsellors for direct intervention services or for consultation purposes with the school staff and students. Individual school administrations determine what constitutes a crisis from their perspective. Crises are identified as being outside the normal realm of events within the school setting, with the potential to create a negative and disruptive impact on the normal functioning of a large part of the student and staff bodies. They are disruptive enough for it to become necessary to stop the regular routine and attend to the crisis. From experience in school crises, an optimal procedure to follow has been delineated (Humphrey et al., 1988; 1990). The first step establishes the time line for tasks. After a school has declared a crisis several meetings are arranged to plan the intervention with the staff and student body. At each of these meetings the correct information on the crisis is determined, those who were involved are identified, and potential strategies for intervention are considered. Meetings are scheduled, from administration and guidance staff, to parents whose children were involved, to teachers, to identified friends, to building staff.

Crises may occur without warning and this procedure is then condensed to cover the very basics. The administration must always be the first contacted. Often a short meeting is held with the administrative staff; it includes teachers who might be most directly involved. Time permitting, the entire teaching staff is informed in a joint session before the start of the school day. No matter how short the available time is, it is of primary importance that everyone (teachers and students) have an accurate understanding of the facts, and that teachers listen for rumours and correct them. Nothing is more destructive during a crisis than the 'rumour mill'. Another important consideration is that one member of staff be designated to talk to the press, and not allow the press to walk through the school, randomly talking to teachers and students.

Depending on the nature of the crisis and who was involved and/or affected by it, special rooms and counsellors are provided for students identified as needing intervention. After the initial crisis, the crisis team meets to evaluate their interventions. Often at this meeting, the team evaluates their resources and makes decisions regarding outside referrals for identified students. They plan a follow-up session in six to nine months to re-evaluate and to identify students still in need of support.

Postvention

Postvention services on the part of the Grief Support and Education Center focus on some type of follow-up services after a significant loss/crisis. Postvention conveys the idea that follow-up interventions of some type may be needed at this time. For example, following an intervention in a school, evaluation should follow within a week, then again at six to nine months. The needs and status of individuals,

staff, and families should be considered based upon present observations. At this time referrals may be made to community resources,
additional education that focuses on different dimensions of the
event may be offered, or supportive services such as a children's or
adolescents' support group may be held during school time.

Working within the school setting can be useful to all concerned,
but care must be taken to follow the requests and agenda of the
school involved. Although we may be experts in a given field, the
educators are the ones who will be left to work with the students.
We cannot risk creating additional problems in a one- or two-hour
classroom intervention. Always take the time to learn as much as
possible about the school population that you will be working with.
Schools differ greatly even within the same geographic area. Issues
of religion, philosophy of education, local school politics, specific
personalities and agendas of teachers involved, types of student, and
parental involvement are some of the variables that need to be
considered before designing a programme.

Churches

Churches have the potential to educate, influence, and support their
members from birth to death. However, a common complaint is that
churches do not provide the needed ongoing support after major
losses, such as death and divorce. Some members and their needs
may not be visible, and some churches may lack understanding and
skills to offer effective support. Bereaved individuals do not have the
energy to seek needed help; and often they have the view that a
church should know their needs and be the initiator of support.
Churches, like friends and families, often offer a general invitation
to call if help is needed. They do not understand that the bereaved
do not have the energy to make a phone call. Even strong people
weary of being strong, and relish the idea of being supported.

Church programmes, designed to educate ministries of consolation, must be tailored to meet the needs of the congregation.
Consideration must be made of the population(s) they wish to
support (e.g. death, divorced, dying); what spiritual viewpoint will
be fostered; how the services will be conducted (e.g. telephone, home
visits, church programmes); and what are their resources (personnel,
time, financial capabilities). As in other programmes and interventions, some basics must be addressed: the understanding of the
categories of loss, the process and tasks of grief, and the need for
support systems and effective coping strategies. Another important
point to keep in mind is that these ministries usually include lay
people, who have varied reasons for becoming involved. Many have

their own unresolved grief issues; some may have a personal mission to change people; and others may want to be supportive, but lack confidence and knowledge. Part of the counsellor's/educator's role is to gain some understanding of the participants and their individual needs for belonging. This is accomplished through experiential activities such as the 'history of loss' and small group sharings after various didactic presentations and videos. The following outlines an example of a five-week training session. Each session lasted for two hours.

Case example: church-based ministry of consolation

This church was in a rural area. The congregation numbered around 500 families. The church members viewed themselves as offering a nurturing environment for those who were members of their congregation. The church building was constructed in 1976 and more than half of the congregation were still the original members. Some years later, the minister believed that the area of loss and grief (as a ministry of support) was lacking. The pastor and the counsellors who would present the training designed the programme. A five-week programme consisting of two-hour sessions was developed. The pastor's personal philosophy was that this was a community need; thus, he invited other ministers and their congregations in the community to participate. The result was that 34 enrolled, 10 representing neighbouring churches. The participants were subsequently divided into four groups in order to share personal reflections and to process the information. A counsellor was assigned to each group to clarify information, to answer specific questions, and to facilitate the interaction of the members.

SESSION 1

Objectives
1. To provide basic information about loss and grief.
2. To provide the opportunity for participants to explore their own issues of loss and grief.

Interventions
1. Participants are asked to introduce themselves and to share their interest in this ministry.
2. Present a 15-minute lecture on the basic concepts and dimensions of loss, grief, and resolution. Use basic information from Chapter 1.
3. Introduce participants to the experiential activity: 'Self-inventory: accommodating to loss and change' (Table 9.3). Instruct them to

Table 9.3   *Self-inventory: accommodating to loss and change*

I.   List three changes or losses that have had a major effect upon your life.
Consider death and non-death events. Also think about symbolic losses or
change that has necessitated a change in your identity (e.g. loss of hopes and
dreams, burnout, graduation, etc.). Also, consider loss of important objects that
served as connections to your past, your heritage, or important people that gave
you a sense of identity and well-being. Lastly, think about losses or unwanted
changes associated with various developmental tasks (e.g. the losses associated
with the responsibilities of having to grow up).

   AGE   LOSS/CHANGES

1.   _____
2.   _____
3.   _____

II. Think about how these losses are affecting you now. You may feel that they
have been fully resolved, and that you are stronger and more fulfilled because of
them; or you might still have unfinished business to cope with; or you may
believe that your life has been negatively changed because of these events. On
the scale below indicate where you are with each change/loss mentioned. Write a
few words to describe your present experience with each.

   No effect   Major effect
   1........2........3........4........5........6........7........8........9........10

1.   ....
2.   ....
3.   ....

III. Choose one of the losses mentioned and discuss how you experienced the process
of grief. Was the process longer and more difficult than you expected? Did you
experience growth? What did you learn about yourself in the course of your
grieving? Any surprises?

---

fill it out individually; then break up into small groups and ask
them to share any part of the exercise they feel comfortable
discussing. Advise them that this exercise has the potential to
trigger painful feelings and that counsellors are available for
support.

Special considerations   Thirty minutes is allotted for the small
group sharing. Often this activity is resisted. Participants' expectations are that they are there to help others, not to look at themselves. This exercise should always be prefaced with the reminder
that no one is exempt from loss and grief; and, in order to minister

to others, it is first important to understand personal losses and possible unresolved issues. It is not possible to minister to others if they have not ministered to themselves first. One group in our experience did not want to end this small group activity after 30 minutes. The activity lasted closer to an hour. Once back in the large group, a spokesperson from each group shared the essence of the content and the affective experience. Further discussion was generated from this sharing. Evaluations from this first session stated that the most important aspect of the evening was the small group sharing. Other groups, however, may prefer the safety of the lecture mode, which involves less personal risk. Evaluations are given after each week to assess the needs of the group and the effectiveness of the material presented.

SESSION 2

Objectives
1. To facilitate an understanding of problems with grief resolution.
2. To identify and address special issues and needs of grieving children.
3. To identify and address special issues and needs of grieving adolescents.

Interventions
1. Present a 15-minute lecture on the difficulties with the resolution of grief. Refer to Chapter 8 for background information.
2. Show the video, *Footsteps on the ceiling* (Phoenix Films, 1981), to introduce the concept of children's unique expression of grief. Instruct participants to discuss cognitive and affective reactions to the video in small groups. Ask each group to have a spokesperson to share reactions with the larger group.
3. Present a 15-minute lecture on the nature and concepts of children's and adolescents' grief. The Appendix to this book includes relevant materials.

Special considerations This session can be difficult because it is often hard to convince well-meaning adults that it is important for children to grieve and not to be overprotected. Time is usually needed to answer many questions regarding the best way to work with grieving children and adolescents. This is also an opportunity to dispel some fears, anxieties, and misinformation. Children must grieve, and on their own timetables. Long-term support systems and adults with effective coping behaviours are significant factors for healthy resolution of childhood and adolescent grief.

SESSION 3

Objectives
1. To understand the nature of family grief.
2. To introduce the concepts of anticipatory grief, especially as it occurs within the context of the family.

Interventions
1. Present a 15-minute lecture on family grief, including anticipatory grief. Chapters 4 and 6 can provide a basis for the information.
2. Show the 30-minute video, *The Ameche family: a family in grief* (Group Two Productions, Inc., 1987). Instruct them to divide up into small groups to process their reactions to the video, and then to have one member from each group give feedback to the larger group. Encourage large group response.
3. Show the 30-minute video, *The death of a gandy dancer* (Learning Corporation of America, 1984). This video illustrates a family involved in anticipatory grief and the concerns of the dying patient.

Special considerations   There may not be sufficient time to show and process two videos. Moreover, the videos usually elicit emotions, and the counsellor may want to provide opportunity for discussion. If this is the case, the *Gandy dancer* video can be eliminated or used at the beginning of the fourth session as an example of communication and listening skills. It has been helpful in the processing of this video to structure the small group discussion by using specific questions. (1) What were the needs of the patient? How did he attempt to communicate them? (2) Did the family help facilitate or hinder the needs of the patient? (3) What did they communicate to the patient? (4) How did each family member address their anticipatory grief? (5) What could they have done differently? (6) How did they change during the process? (7) As members of a church outreach ministry how could you effectively intervene with this family?

SESSION 4

Objectives
1. To present information on more effective styles of communicating and listening.
2. To provide an opportunity for participants to evaluate personal skills of listening and communication.
3. To practise these skills through role play.

Interventions
1. Present general information for 20 minutes on listening and communication skills.
2. Instruct participants to fill out an evaluation of their listening habits (Table 9.4) in order to assess personal strengths and limitations that can be addressed during role plays.
3. Divide into small groups of three and facilitate role plays.

Special considerations This session is highly interactive, consisting mostly of opportunities for role plays that allow participants the opportunity to practise listening and communication skills within a learning environment. The didactic presentation lasts 20 to 30 minutes and includes information (with handouts) on levels of communication, guidelines to communication skills and better listening, and observing verbal and nonverbal communications. General information on communication and listening can be used for this session. The evaluation of listening habits (Table 9.4) is done alone and thus does not produce a risk. In private, members can become cognizant of areas that need attention. Many become aware that they have been quick to offer advice based on their beliefs and values, yet negligent in listening. Remind the group that no matter how similar a situation might seem to their own, it will always be unique to that individual. It can never be assumed that the innermost reality of another human being can ever be fully understood.

For the role plays three-person groups are used. Written scripts are given to the helpee and the helper. The helper is given basic information about the helpee and the type of loss involved. A number of different losses should be included in the role plays, in order to acquaint the group with numerous possibilities that they might encounter in their ministry. The person acting as the helpee is given some detail about his or her loss, in order to make the role more realistic. The observer is instructed to watch the interaction for nonverbal signs of communication and to assess the comfort level of both role-players. The role play lasts for about 10 minutes. Enough time must be allotted in order to understand the nature of the problem and to allow sufficient time for practising communication and listening skills. First the observer asks each how the experience was for them in the particular role that they had been assigned, and then presents his or her observations; this facilitates a three-way discussion. Recommendations are made, and the counsellors are available for input. This activity takes about one and a half hours of the session, and everyone has an opportunity to practise each role.

Table 9.4   *Evaluating listening habits*

	TICK ONE		
	Almost always	Occasionally	Seldom
In a listening situation I:			
Face the speaker and sit close enough to hear			
Interrupt or jump in			
Rehearse my answer while the person is speaking			
Think (while listening) about other things			
Listen to the feelings being expressed so as to better understand the comments			
Determine my own bias			
Watch the nonverbal behaviour, gestures, etc., to gain a deeper understanding			
Look for the true meanings underlying the remarks			
Maintain good eye contact			
Stop the person talking when I do not understand something, and ask him/her to explain			

SESSION 5

Objectives
1. To continue to practise skills of listening and communication.
2. To discuss the administrative components of a ministry of consolation.

Interventions
1. Continue role plays, using a 'round robin' technique and base the interventions on a family, instead of an individual.
2. Facilitate a determination of goals and objectives of the programme and assumption of responsibilities through large group discussion and 'brainstorming'.

Special considerations The final week continues the practice of role plays. These role plays are based in family settings, and done in a 'round robin' approach. A number of family cases were designed, focusing on losses such as death, illness, divorce, and retirement. Volunteers are recruited to play the roles of different family members in each of the case examples, and approximately five for each case example are recruited to play the helper roles. The 'round robin' approach utilizes more than one person as the helper. The group of helpers are instructed to sit in a semicircle facing the family, and to take turns intervening. After one helper has four or five exchanges, another helper is invited to pick up where the first has left off, or to follow a new line of inquiry or support. The value of this approach is that the helpers learn from each other, and when they are observers they can listen more attentively and become more aware of nuances in communication. There is a sense of nervousness and intensity when one is in the role of helper; a helper may be so focused on one area that a broader perspective may be missed. Participants seem to prefer this type of role playing and seem to be able to become more involved in the actual roles and the subsequent processing.

The last 30 minutes of this final session is spent discussing administrative components of the outreach programme. Members have to determine initial goals and objectives for the programme, set time lines for follow-up meetings to implement the programme, and decide on those who will accept the various responsibilities for meetings and organizational needs. Counsellors offer ongoing availability for future consultation, and it is important that these decisions are made, with firm commitments before this session ends. Handouts offering organizational plans (Table 9.5) are included in this session and reference is made to them; however, they are not gone over in detail.

Nursing home settings

Education in this setting is for those professionals who are involved in the care of the elderly, primarily in a residential milieu. This is an important and often neglected area of professional education. Placement in a nursing home has often been viewed as a warehousing prelude to the end of one's life. Most people do not leave the nursing home and return to the community to live independently. The needs of the residents, other than for physical care, are often not known. Until recently, the fact that a nursing home placement, in itself, was a loss had not been validated. Those in a nursing home have immediately incurred many losses upon entry, will accrue more

Table 9.5   *Church outreach programme: organizational chart*

Goals and objectives	Responsibility	Proposed completion date	Completed date
To identify grieving persons within the congregation	Initial identification		
To establish and activate an Identification Process Committee according to suggested responsibilities	Establish Identification Committee		
To establish and activate Telephone Network System Committee	Establish a Telephone Committee		
To establish and activate a Home Visit Committee	Establish a Home Visit Programme		
To provide additional supportive programmes within the church	Establish church programmes		
To be a source of referral to community agencies as needed	Establish a referral system		
Programmes for volunteers	Establish programmes for volunteers		

during their stay, and will often use idle time in this setting to dwell upon and despair over a multitude of losses incurred throughout their lifetime. Attention must be given to all these issues: lives need to be validated as having been meaningful and worthwhile, and lives that still need to be lived must be empowered.

Workshops (six hours or more) have been given to educate professionals who work with this population. The day begins with basic information about loss in life, grief, and bereavement. Chapters 1 and 2 can be used for background information on the broader topic and for assessment and intervention strategies to be used with the residents. Information from Chapters 4, 6, 7, and 8 will be valuable when assessments indicate issues of family, antici-patory grief, specific deaths (e.g. suicide, AIDS, neonatal), or past unresolved losses that currently need closure. Information presented in this type of a workshop must include a wide range of possible losses that may have spanned a lifetime. The discussion in Chapter 1 regarding the 'Perspectives' and the chart used as a counselling tool in Chapter 3 (Table 3.1, p. 44) will be useful in this setting!

Included in this training must be an opportunity for participants to become aware of their own losses and how they have coped with them. An experiential exercise that addresses personal loss (Table 9.3, p. 168) is valuable for raising personal insight and exploring support for the helping professional. Issues of professional burnout must be addressed, and sufficient time allowed to explore solutions. Often these workshops promote support among the participants, and a positive experience will encourage commitments for future attention to personal needs.

The afternoon of this workshop identifies more specifically the losses and issues of the residents, and possible ways to facilitate empowerment. Raphael (1983) discussed this:

> The griefs of growing old begin when an individual first realizes that he or she cannot do, with ease, something that before this was easily accomplished without thought. It also begins when one realizes that one will not, now, achieve the fullness of one's hopes and dreams; that one's life is not limitless, but finite, and that the remaining time is not great. (1983: 283)

Taken from her work and included in discussion are various losses, such as loss of vision, hearing, sexual function, body part, health and well-being, brain function, meaningful work, and multiple roles and relationships. Each loss is discussed and participants are asked to reflect upon their residents' losses and share specific examples. Not only does this discussion raise awareness; it also encourages exploration and understanding of the deeper meaning of these losses in the lives of the residents.

In addition to these types of loss, discussion also addresses issues of loss within a residential setting. This is introduced by asking members to participate in a forced-choice activity. They are instructed to take an 8×11 inch piece of paper and fold it into six equal parts. In each section they are asked to write present, meaningful roles. Examples of roles that are identified are those of spouse, worker, parent, child, friend, and volunteer. Then they are instructed to eliminate one of these roles. The activity continues until they are forced to decide between the last two. This exercise heightens awareness and feelings associated with loss of freedom and personal control in life. If they have not been empathetic or aware of this in the lives of the residents, it is a very a poignant experience.

Discussion then moves to lack of choice within an institutional setting. A few examples are given, such as no choice of food, room-mates, activities; then participants are asked to cite examples they have in their settings, with possible ideas for increasing the range of choice. One nursing home administrator stated that a choice could be as simple as asking a person what type of socks he would like to have. He recalled an incident with one of the male residents over a pair of socks that could easily have been resolved, but instead became a major incident involving a number of the staff. This gentleman had no living family to provide some of the basic clothing items or personal care supplies. When a situation like this occurs in the facility, these items and supplies are assigned to people out of a general supply that is purchased or donated. When it became apparent that this man had no socks, a pair was automatically provided from the supply closet. The man stated that he did not like that colour of socks. This was ignored and he was told that he had no say in this matter. Consequently, he became very agitated and verbally abusive to several of the nearby staff, resulting in the need to sedate him. In retrospect, the administrator came to understand one individual's basic human need for personal choice and respect. Time permitting, a video is shown to further reinforce these concepts. *The death of a gandy dancer* (Learning Corporation of America, 1984) is a useful video which portrays the needs and struggles of an elderly man to have personal control and choices and to expect honesty and respect from those around him. Although it does not take place within a nursing home, the issues are pertinent for discussion. Prior to viewing the video, participants are instructed to listen for various losses, the need for personal control and choices, validation of a past life, and choices that were made to enable empowerment.

The final part of this seminar is used to identify ways to promote integration of lifetime experiences and to promote new choices and empowerment within a structured, institutional setting. The majority of those who have attended these workshops believe in the concepts proposed; they learn from the programme and have their beliefs and ideas confirmed and seem more normal. The final part of the programme offers the opportunity to share ideas that they may already have conceived, but never verbalized. The didactic component of this final portion focuses on ideas for various types of programmes, activities, or groups that can be offered in this setting. Potential groups include reminiscing, remotivation, specific deaths, losses over a lifetime, and family groups. Many who enter a nursing home do so following the death of a spouse. Identifying those who have lost a spouse prior to their placement provides the opportunity to offer a support group such as the one proposed in Chapter 5. Information for development and implementation for other groups, such as the reminiscing group, can be found in professional literature. One excellent resource is a book written by Burnside, a specialist with this population who has written *Working with the elderly: group process and techniques* (1994). This provides data from research to specifics for assessment, group formation and implementation.

Working within the nursing home has seldom been viewed as a positive experience. Burnout and lack of empathy have often been the hallmarks of this occupation. It is always difficult to work with a population and realize that this could very well be one's own future. There are few other work settings that offer such a stark and potential reality for the professional caregiver. Many fulfil the basic requirements of the job and do not become overly involved personally or professionally. The purpose of this training is to reframe the professional experience into a more positive one, and move towards a transformation of a bleak encounter into a growth-promoting one. According to Ivey:

> Life is simultaneously a journey, a destination, and a state of being. The journey is development; the destination is an inevitable repetition of our return to where we began (but with a new state of awareness); and the state of being is our ontology, our total experience of the past, present, and future. (1986: 3)

Old age and change continue to be part of the journey. Development is a continuous process until death. The mental health professional has a moral and ethical obligation to be aware of this and to be committed to action on the basis of this belief.

The corporate world

Crisis intervention programmes and education for employers and employees (similar to the school outreach programmes) are valuable interventions in the workplace. In the United States an increasing number of businesses are establishing employee assistance programmes that identify problems and offer treatment for a number of issues. The majority of the professionals, however, are not trained in loss and bereavement, and do not understand that the underlying factors in many problems of their employees are loss-related. Many employees are transferred to drug and alcohol programmes, without an in-depth assessment to identify contributing factors. The purpose of this section on corporations is to address a specific issue that has become a social concern of the last two decades and will continue into the new century: downsizing and restructuring, and their implications for loss and grieving.

In postindustrial American society, a large number of employees have been affected by corporate restructuring. Many have been encouraged to retire early, and many others lacking seniority have been terminated in the process of downsizing. Loss is apparent for those who have retired or have become unemployed; however, it is not as apparent, nor is it often validated, for those whose positions have been restructured and who are attempting to cope with loss and grief in terms of altered work-related roles and identities. Although many corporate settings have addressed certain aspects of change (e.g. finances, retraining), the grief reactions have been ignored, negated, or viewed as a sign of weakness.

Schlenker and Gutek (1987) have explored loss of work and professional roles. Professionals (no matter what the occupation) spend many years in roles that confirm a core sense of their identities. When changes occur in these roles and resolution is not the outcome, the results are lowered satisfaction with work, lowered self-esteem, and depression. These are the same effects found in people who lose their jobs. The effects of restructuring and downsizing are often overlooked because the prevalent dictum is that one should be grateful that one is still employed. 'Survivors' of corporate re-organization (i.e. those who remain) realize loss and grief. Although they did not lose employment, they have experienced high levels of anxiety, guilt, anger, depression, and a loss of commitment (Pliner, 1990).

Corporations are facing the challenge of competing in a global economy. Yesterday's solutions have become today's problems. The corporate career (Goeffee & Scase, 1992) was a reality during the postwar decades. Managers worked within corporate hierarchies and expected promotion, increasing salaries, status, and security. Post-industrial society presents a different reality: flexibility and the necessity to be a member of a team are corporate priorities; corporate commitment is not to individual loyalty but to its own survival.

When corporations expect to downsize or restructure, planning includes economic projections, proposed corporate changes, marketing strategies, comparisons with similar companies, and other business-oriented information and action. In such a heavily data-oriented and cognitively based context, many would not view as valid a concern for grief on the part of the surviving employees. And yet, consideration of their welfare is crucial to organizational survival.

A workshop to address the needs and issues of employees who remain after restructuring or downsizing will be soundly based in theoretical concepts of human behaviour. As with other educational outreach programmes, a general understanding of loss (over a lifetime), grief, the bereavement process, and the influence of past (and often unresolved) losses must be presented. The chart on

'Perspectives' (Table 3.1. p. 44), discussed in prior chapters, is an excellent educational tool in this type of programme, as it heightens the awareness of the impact of this type of loss across various human dimensions. Corporations often view the grief response as an indicator of weakness, because they have little understanding of the issues inherent in career role loss and change. Once the pervasive nature of loss has been validated, education and/or intervention can address areas of needed change in the workplace. Change may be mandatory and involve little choice on the part of the individual employee; however, corporations need to understand that they will benefit more in the future if they consider compromise, accommodation, and involvement of individuals in decision-making for purposeful change. Within this workshop, the above concepts are presented with specific examples (real or hypothetical) highlighting the corporation involved. The theories and concepts of this programme will be accepted only when they can be shown to be directly relevant to the particular corporate structure being addressed, and worthwhile to consider because of future economic survival and success.

Coping with imposed change is another basic tenet of this workshop. Coping often is interpreted to mean blindly accepting or stoically enduring adversity. Effective coping strategies are often unknown, and all presentations on loss must include a broader understanding of the nature of stress and coping. Information in Chapter 5 regarding stress and coping can be incorporated in this part of the presentation. Following this, the workshop can conclude with the discussion focusing on employee assistance programmes that address the psychological needs of individuals, lifestyle changes outside the work setting, and opportunities for employees to regain a sense of choice and personal control in their lives.

Many, in the course of their lives, will be involved in the institutions that were discussed in this chapter. These institutions are made up of individuals who have and who will continue to have loss and grief throughout their lifetime. Moreover, many of these institutions may be or become the source of one's loss and grief. Identification of losses in these institutions and providing the opportunity for education and outreach services can prove a positive contribution in the mental health field now and in the future.

References

American Psychiatric Association (1994). *Diagnostic and statistical manual of mental disorders* (4th ed.). Washington, DC: APA.

Attig, T. (1992). *Relearning the world*. Paper presented at the annual bereavement seminar of the Grief Support and Education Center, Canton, Ohio, October.

Beck, A.T. (1978). *Beck Depression Inventory*. Philadelphia, PA: Centre for Cognitive Therapy.

Becker, E. (1973). *The denial of death*. New York: The Free Press.

Bowen, M. (1974). Toward the differentiation of self in one's family of origin. In F. Andres & J. Lorio (Eds.), *Georgetown family symposium, Vol. 1*. Washington, DC: Department of Psychiatry, Georgetown University Medical Center.

Bowen, M. (1978). *Family therapy in clinical practice*. New York: Jason Aronson.

Bowlby, J. (1969). *Attachment and loss: Vol. 1. Attachment*. New York: Basic Books.

Bowlby, J. (1973). *Attachment and loss: Vol. 2. Separation: Anxiety and anger*. New York: Basic Books.

Bowlby, J. (1980). *Attachment and loss: Vol. 3. Loss: Sadness and depression*. New York: Basic Books.

Brayer, M.M. (1977). The spiritual component. In N. Linzer (Ed.), *Understanding bereavement and grief* (pp. 47–72). New York: Yeshiva University Press.

Burnside, I. (1994). *Working with the elderly: Group process and techniques* (2nd ed.). Monterey, CA: Wadsworth Health Sciences.

Cattell, R.B., Krug, S.E., & Sheier, I.H. (1976). *IPAT Anxiety Scale Questionnaire: Handbook*. Champaign, IL: Institute for Personality and Ability Testing.

Clark, A. (1985). Grief and gestalt therapy. *The Gestalt Journal, 1*, 49–63.

Corr, C. (1991). *Care of the terminally ill*. Paper presented at the Association of Death Education and Counseling 13th Annual Conference, Duluth, MN.

Davidson, M. (1983). *Uncommon sense: The life and thought of Ludwig von Bertalanffy*. Los Angeles: J.P. Tarcher.

Davies, B. (1990). Long-term follow-up of bereaved siblings. In J.D. Morgan (Ed.), *The dying and the bereaved teenager* (pp. 78–79). Philadelphia, PA: The Charles Press.

Day, B. (1992). *Suicide: The ultimate abandonment*. Paper presented at the Association of Death Education and Counseling 14th Annual Conference, Boston, MA, March.

Demi, A.S., & Miles, M. (1987). Parameters of normal grief: A Delphi study. *Death Studies, 11*, 397–412.

Deutsch, H. (1937). Absence of grief. *Psychoanalytic Quarterly, 6*, 12–22.

Doka, K. (Ed.). (1989). *Disenfranchised grief: Recognizing hidden sorrow*. Lexington, MA: Lexington Books.

Duvall, E.M., & Miller, B.C. (1985). *Marriage and family development* (6th ed.). New York: Harper & Row.

Engel, G. (1961). Is grief a disease? A challenge for medical research. *Psychosomatic Medicine, 23*, 18–22.

Erikson, E.H. (1968). *Identity, youth and crisis.* New York: Norton.

Fox, S. (1991). *Grieving children and adolescents.* Workshop presented by National Center for Death Education, Newton, MA, July.

Freud, S. (1957). *Mourning and melancholia.* In J. Strachey (Ed. and Trans.), *The standard edition of the complete psychological works of Sigmund Freud* (Vol. 14). London: Hogarth. (Original work published 1914).

Fulton, R.F. (1977). General aspects. In N. Linzer (Ed.), *Understanding bereavement and grief* (pp. 3–9). New York: Yeshiva University Press.

Glasser, W. (1990). *Control theory.* New York: Harper & Row.

Glick, I.O., Weiss, R.S., & Parkes, C.M. (1974). *The first year of bereavement.* New York: Wiley.

Goeffee, R., & Scase, R. (1992), Organizational change and the corporate career: The restructuring of managers' job aspirations. *Human Relations, 45*, 363–385.

Group Two Productions, Inc. (Producer). (1987). *The Ameche family: A family in grief* (video). (Available from Research Press, Champaign, IL).

Haley, J. (1980). *Leaving home: The therapy of disturbed young people.* New York: McGraw-Hill.

Horowitz, M., Wilner, N., & Alvarez, W. (1979). Impact of Events Scale: A measure of subjective stress. *Psychosomatic Medicine, 41* (3), 209–218.

Horowitz, M.J., Wilner, N., Marmar, C., & Krupnick, J. (1980). Pathological grief and the activation of latent self-images. *American Journal of Psychiatry, 137*, 1157–1162.

Humphrey, G.M., Klena, L., & Davis-Harper, C. (1988). *Units on grief and loss for use with children and adolescents in the school setting* (Vol. 1, No. 1). North Canton, OH: The Grief Support and Education Center.

Humphrey, G.M., Harper, C.D., & Bridges, V. (1990). *Units on grief and loss for use with children and adolescents in the school setting* (Vol. 1, No. 2). North Canton, OH: The Grief Support and Education Center.

Ivey, A.E. (1986). *Developmental therapy.* San Francisco: Jossey-Bass.

Jackson, D.D. (1965). Family rules: Marital quid pro quo. *Archives of General Psychiatry, 12*, 589–594.

Jackson, E. (1977). The spiritual component. In N. Linzer (Ed.), *Understanding bereavement and grief* (pp. 78–79). New York: Yeshiva University Press.

Kennell, J.H., & Klaus, M.H. (1976). *Maternal infant bonding.* St Louis: C.V. Mosby.

Krementz, J. (1989). You always have to have hope: How it feels to fight for your life. *Family Circle*, September, 88–92.

Kubler-Ross, E. (1969). *On death and dying.* New York: Macmillan.

Kubler-Ross, E. (1975). *Death: The final stage of growth.* New York: Macmillan.

Learning Corporation of America. (Producer). (1984). *The death of a gandy dancer* (video). (Available from Coronet/MTI, Northbrook, IL).

Lindemann, E. (1944). Symptomatology and management of acute grief. *American Journal of Psychiatry, 101*, 141–148.

Madanes, C. (1981). *Strategic family therapy.* San Francisco: Jossey-Bass.

Minuchin, S. (1974). *Families and family therapy.* Cambridge, MA: Harvard University Press.

Nichols, J.A. (1986). Newborn death. In T. Rando (Ed.), *Parental loss of a child* (pp. 145–157). Champaign, IL: Research Press.

Nichols, M.P., & Schwartz, R.C. (1991). *Family therapy: Concepts and methods* (2nd ed.). Boston: Allyn & Bacon.

Parkes, C.M., & Weiss, R.S. (1983) *Recovery from bereavement.* New York: Basic Books.

Phoenix Films. (Producer). (1981). *Footsteps on the ceiling* (video). (Available from Phoenix Films, Inc., New York).

Pliner, J. (1990). Staying with or leaving the organization. *Prevention in Human Services, 8,* 159–177.

Rando, T.A. (1983). An investigation of grief and adaptation in parents whose children have died from cancer. *Journal of Pediatric Psychology, 8,* 3–20.

Rando, T.A. (1984). *Grief, dying, and death: Clinical interventions for caregivers.* Champaign, IL: Research Press.

Rando, T.A. (Ed.). (1986). *Loss and anticipatory grief.* Lexington, MA: Lexington Books.

Rando, T.A. (1988). *Grieving: How to go on living when someone you love dies.* Lexington, MA: Lexington Books.

Rando, T.A. (1993). *Treatment of complicated mourning.* Champaign, IL: Research Press.

Raphael, B. (1983). *The anatomy of bereavement.* New York: Basic Books.

Raphael, B. (1992). *Counseling after catastrophic loss.* Paper presented at the Association of Death Education and Counseling 14th Annual Conference, Boston, MA, March.

Redmond, L. (1989). *Surviving: When someone you love was murdered.* Clearwater, FL: Psychological Consultation and Education Services.

Rotter, S.B. (1966). Generalized expectancies for internal vs. external control of reinforcement. *Psychological Monographs, 80* (1), (Whole No. 609).

Rynearson, E. (1990). Pathological grief: The queen's croquet ground. *Psychiatric Annals, 20,* 295–303.

Schlenker, J.A., & Gutek, B.A. (1987). Effects of role loss on work-related attitudes. *Journal of Applied Psychology, 72,* 287–293.

Sprenkle, D.H., & Piercy, F.P. (1992). A family therapy informed view of the current state of the family in the United States. *Family Relations, 41,* 404–408.

Stephenson, J.S. (1985). *Death, grief, and mourning.* New York: The Free Press.

West, J. (1994). *Family therapy.* Lecture presented in Family Therapy course, ACHVE Department, School of Education, Kent State University, Kent, Ohio, March.

Wisensale, S.K. (1992). Toward the 21st century: Family change and public policy. *Family Relations, 41,* 417–422.

Worden, J.W. (1991). *Grief counseling and grief therapy: A handbook for the mental health practitioner* (2nd ed.). New York: Springer.

Yalom, I.D. (1985). *The theory and practice of group psychotherapy* (3rd ed.). New York: Basic Books.

Zimmerman, S.L. (1992). Family trends: What implications for family policy? *Family Relations, 41,* 423–429.

Zimpfer, D.G. (1992). Psychosocial treatment of life-threatening disease: A wellness model. *Journal of Counseling & Development, 71,* 203–209.

Appendix
Resources on Dying, Death, and Grieving

Books for professionals

Cook, A.S., & Dworkin, D.S. (1992). *Helping the bereaved: Therapeutic interventions for children, adolescents, and adults*. New York: Basic Books.

The authors present examples of working with the bereaved. They stress the need for clinicians to individualize intervention, especially for nonwhites, who may have differing values about death. They also expect self-awareness on the part of the therapist. Assessment methods, the process of intervention, and recommendations for considering group or individual therapy are provided.

Cox, G.R., & Fundis, R.J. (Eds). (1992). *Spiritual, ethical, and pastoral aspects of death and bereavement*. Amityville, NY: Baywood.

This volume assists caregivers in arriving at acceptable ethical positions in their pastoral, counselling, medical, and mortician roles. Spiritual and ethical aspects are considered. Attention is given to ministry to people with AIDS, to children's experience with death, and to spiritual care in hospices. Discussion includes euthanasia, organ transplants, neonatal death, and other issues.

Doka, K.J., with Morgan, J.D. (1993). *Death and spirituality*. Amityville, NY: Baywood.

This volume deals with understanding the norms of various religious traditions and the religious and spiritual issues that may arise in illness and bereavement. Counselling discussion includes work with the dying, spiritual crisis in bereavement, rituals and beliefs, spiritual care of the traumatized, suicide, and AIDS.

Dunne, E.J., McIntosh, J.L., & Maxim, K.D. (Eds). (1987). *Suicide and its aftermath: Understanding and counseling the survivors*. Dunmore, PA: W.W. Norton.

Hope and compassion for suicide survivors are offered and specific ideas for caregivers on how to understand and respond to families in the aftermath of suicide.

Dyregrov, A. (1991). *Grief in children: A handbook for adults*. Bristol, PA and London: Jessica Kingsley.

This is useful for teachers, counsellors, pastoral workers, parents, and others faced with the task of understanding children in grief and trying to help them.

Haasl, B., & Marnocha, J. (1990). *Bereavement support group program for children*. Muncie, IN: Accelerated Development.

This is a five-session bereavement support programme to use with children, with details of purposes, materials, and specific activities. The leader manual contains rationale, objectives, and procedures. The participant workbook includes fill-in activities and information for the children.

Hendriks, J.H., Black, D., & Kaplan, T. (1993). *When father kills mother: Guiding children through trauma and grief.* London: Routledge.

This is a sensitive reading to help professionals work with one who endures the impact of a simultaneous murder and parental loss. Trauma and confusion are compounded by fear, guilt, and/or anger.

Jarratt, C.J. (1994). *Helping children cope with separation and loss* (Rev. ed.). Boston, MA: Harvard Common Press.

Death, adoption, foster care, abandonment, and divorce have great impact on children. This book shows the child's grief process. Counsellors learn how to tell a child about a loss, how to understand and support grief, how to help children respond to their emotions, how to deal with problems of self-esteem and control, and how to help the child eventually to let go and move on.

Activities and props such as puppets, drawings, journals, and rituals are included. Issues such as getting stuck in mourning and recycling loss are discussed.

Kubler-Ross, E. (1973). *On death and dying.* London: Routledge.

A classic text for nurses, doctors, clergy and others working with the dying.

LaGrand, L.E. (1986). *Coping with separation and loss as a young adult.* Springfield, IL: Charles Thomas.

Covers major types of loss in the lives of young adults, coping mechanisms, managing grief, and interventions. Based on the author's research with young adults.

Lendrum, S., & Syme, G. (1992). *The gift of tears.* London: Routledge.

Designed to help people who find that they have to cope, in the course of their work or daily lives, with the grief of others. The authors use theory, accessible case histories and exercises to involve the reader.

Locke, S.A. (1990). *Coping with loss: A guide for caregivers.* Springfield, IL: Charles Thomas.

This volume focuses on loss in the health-care setting: trauma or death in the emergency room, life-threatening illness, loss associated with reproduction, children and loss, the elderly and loss.

Mogenson, G. (1992). *Greeting the angels: An imaginal view of the mourning process.* Amityville, NY: Baywood.

This book, in the genre of Imaginal Psychology, introduces 'angels', the interior figures who greet the bereaved during the mourning process in reverie and dream. As the bereaved person enters into a relationship with these images, grief becomes individualized. In a process which may become spiritual (but not necessarily religious), the therapist draws on dreams, biographical fragments, poetry, psychoanalysis, and Jungian psychology.

Murray Parkes, C. (1996). *Bereavement: Studies of grief in adult life* (3rd ed.). London: Routledge.

A seminal study into the effects and scientific understanding of bereavement based on 12 years work with widows.

Oates, M.D. (1993). *Death in the school community: A handbook for counselors, teachers and administrators*. Alexandria, VA: American Counseling Association (5999 Stevenson Ave, 22304). (USA).

For counsellors, teachers, and administrators who must be prepared to respond to tragedy in their school, this book provides a step-by-step action plan and techniques for coping with post-traumatic stress disorder. It also explains the grief process in children and adolescents, healthy grief responses, and how to lead loss and grief groups. Case studies, various materials and forms are provided.

O'Toole, D. (1988). *Bridging the bereavement gap* (2nd ed.). Burnsville, NC: Rainbow Connection.

A comprehensive manual for preparing and programming hospice bereavement services.

Pennells, M., & Smith, S.C. (1995). *The forgotten mourners: Guidelines for working with bereaved children*. London and Washington, DC: Jessica Kingsley/Taylor & Francis.

This volume helpfully addresses the specific issues and methods that relate to younger bereaved.

Rando, T.A. (1993). *Treatment of complicated mourning*. Champaign, IL: Research Press.

This volume focuses on pathological, unresolved, or abnormal grief. It provides caregivers with practical therapeutic strategies and interventions to use when traditional grief counselling is insufficient.

Rosen, E.J. (1990). *Families facing death: Family dynamics of terminal illness*. Lexington, MA: Lexington Books.

This is a guide for those who are trying to help families through the struggle of living with dying. The purpose is to find principles for understanding why families behave as they do and how they can be helped. Examples are offered of families who confronted loss successfully as well as some that did not. It doesn't moralize, nor does it merely present sterile data.

Roth, D., & LeVier, E. (Eds). (1990). *Being human in the face of death*. Santa Monica, CA: IBS Press.

This book can help caregivers who work with dying people unlock one of the best resources they have: their humanness. The focus is on the dying process, and on the function that caregivers can play in being present for a dying person and in being able to facilitate communication between patient and family members. Includes training resources for caregivers.

Staudacher, C. (1991). *Men and grief: A guide for men surviving the death of a loved one*. Oakland, CA: New Harbinger.

This volume explores the unique patterns of male bereavement. Based on extensive interviews with male survivors, it describes the characteristics of male grief, explains the forces that influence it, and provides step-by-step help for the male survivor. It is presented both as a guide for men surviving the death of a loved one and a resource for caregivers and mental health professionals.

Wolfelt, A. (1988). *Death and grief: A guide for clergy*. Muncie, IN: Accelerated Development.

Focuses on adult grief, with special emphasis on the role of clergy in bereavement care.

Worden, J.W. (1991) *Grief counseling and grief therapy: A handbook for the mental health practitioner* (2nd ed.). New York: Springer, and London: Routledge.

Mental health professionals can help clients cope with both normal and abnormal grief. Details the mechanisms of normal grief and the procedures for helping clients accomplish the 'tasks of mourning'. The author explains how unresolved grief can lead to problems requiring psychotherapy, and how the therapist can diagnose and treat exaggerated, chronic, masked, and delayed grief reactions.

Books on loss including death

Aiken, L.R. (1994). *Dying, death, and bereavement* (3rd ed.). Boston: Allyn & Bacon.

A comprehensive and interdisciplinary survey of research, writing, and professional practices concerned with death and dying. It is a review of thanatology, including cultural beliefs and practices, human development and death, moral and legal issues, treatment of the dying and the dead, and bereavement and widowhood. Contains material on abortion, euthanasia, and AIDS.

Corless, I.B., Germino, B.B., & Pittman, M. (1994). *Dying, death, and bereavement: Theoretical perspectives and other ways of knowing*. Boston: Jones & Bartlett.

Presents six chapters on aspects of death and dying, and 11 chapters on thanatology. A unique section gives a critical interpretation of several images of death from the literary and visual arts in an effort to explore the universal experience that underlies both traditional and nontraditional forms of mourning.

Counts, D.R., & Counts, D.A. (Eds). (1991). *Coping with the final tragedy: Cultural variation in dying and grieving*. Amityville, NY: Baywood.

This book emphasizes common concerns shared by all humanity while at the same time emphasizing cultural diversities and the variety in the ways that people experience death and grief.

DeSpelder, L.A., & Strickland, A.L. (1992). *The last dance: Encountering death and dying* (3rd ed.). Mountain View, CA: Mayfield.

Diverse points of view on death and dying are presented to examine the assumptions, orientations, and predispositions that have limited discussion for decades. The book's theme is that unbiased investigation will make choices available which otherwise might be neglected due to prejudice or ignorance.

Dickinson, D., & Johnson, M. (1993). *Death, dying and bereavement*. London: Sage.

A collection of separate writings expressing diverse viewpoints on the human issues surrounding death.

Doka, K.J. (Ed.). (1989). *Disenfranchised grief: Recognizing hidden sorrow*. Lexington, MA: Lexington Books.

Researchers and mental health care professionals explore instances in which grief is an entirely natural response to loss and yet because the loss is not openly acknowledged, socially sanctioned, or publicly shared, the mourner is deprived of emotional release and the support that shared grief can bring.

Littlewood, J. (1992). *Aspects of grief: Bereavement in adult life*. London: Routledge.

Looks at the importance of support networks, both family and professional, and how society's attitudes affect our ability to cope.

Marris, P. (1986). *Loss and change*. (Rev. ed.). London: Routledge.

Discusses social change and the diffusion of innovations that have influenced our lives. Bereavement is treated as a special form of loss.

Rando, T.A. (Ed.). (1986). *Loss and anticipatory grief*. Lexington, MA: Lexington Books.

Rando's intent is to utilize the forewarning of a loss in a positive and creative way. The general argument is that premature detachment from the dying person, poor communication, lack of appropriate acts, and failure to close the relationship predispose the survivor to a poor bereavement outcome.

Rickgarn, R.L.V. (1994). *Perspectives on college suicide*. Amityville, NY: Baywood.

With the words of college students themselves about their suicidal experience, the reader learns the effect suicide has upon individuals and the campus as a whole. Information on suicide rate, suicide prevention programmes, antecedents and aetiology of suicide, and intervention procedures are offered, so that both paraprofessionals and professionals will gain insight and information on how to act appropriately to suicide incidence on campus.

Wertheimer, A. (1986). *A special scar: The experiences of people bereaved by suicide*. London: Routledge.

This book places special emphasis on understanding family relationships as they have been affected by a loved one's self-inflicted death.

Zisook, S. (Ed.). (1987). *Biopsychosocial aspects of bereavement*. Washington, DC: American Psychiatric Press.

This book distinguishes between 'normal' and pathological grief. Includes the varied reasons for an individual crossing the boundary, spousal grief and adjustment to widowhood, inventories and measures of grief and distress, and psychoendocrine and immune functions during bereavement.

Organizations

American Association of Grief Counselors, Inc. 15345 Dix-Toledo Road, Southgate, MI 48195, USA. Telephone (800) 796–4333.

This organization promotes the work and function of professional grief counsellors and actively supports their endeavours through education, networking, and public relations.

American Association of Suicidology. 2459 South Ash, Denver, CO, USA. Telephone (303) 692–0985.

Education organization that serves as a national clearing house on suicide.

Association for Death Education and Counseling. 638 Prospect Avenue, Hartford, CT 06105, USA. Telephone (203) 586–7503.

A nonprofit educational, professional, and scientific organization devoted to the promotion and upgrading of the quality of death education and death-related counselling. Annual conference.

Children's Hospice International. 1101 King Street, #131, Alexandria, VA 22314, USA. Telephone (800) 24-CHILD.

CHI provides a support system and resource bank for health care professionals, families, and organizations that offer hospice care to terminally ill children.

CLIMB, Inc. (Center for Loss in Multiple Birth). PO Box 3696, Oak Brook, IL 60522, USA.

International network. Support by and for parents who have experienced the death of one or more of their children during a multiple pregnancy, at birth, or in infancy or childhood. Telephone support, information on the grieving process, monthly chapter meetings. National newsletter and sibling newsletter. Chapter leader's manual. Resource library.

Compassionate Friends. Box 1347, Oak Brook, IL 60521, USA. Telephone (708) 990–0010.

Nationwide (in USA) self-help support groups for parents who have experienced the death of a child from any cause at any age. Newsletter.

Cot Death Research and Support for Bereaved Parents, 8a Alexandra Parade, Weston Super Mare, UK. Telephone 01836 219010.

A full counselling service to newly bereaved parents following the unexpected death of their baby.

CRUSE-Bereavement Care, Cruse House, 126 Sheen Road, Richmond, Surrey TW9 1UR, UK. Telephone 0181 940 4818.

A registered charity offering counselling, information and support through nearly 200 branches in the UK.

Gay Bereavement Project, Vaughan M. Williams Centre, Colindale Hospital, London NW9 5GH, UK. Telephone 0181 455 8894.

Telephone counselling for those bereaved by death of same-sex life partner.

National Hospice Organization. 1901 N. Moore Street, Arlington, VA 22209, USA. Telephone (703) 243–5900.

Maintains resource and referral information for persons who are dying.

National Sudden Infant Death Syndrome (SIDS) Foundation. 10500 Little Putuxent Parkway, Suite 420, Columbia, MD 21044, USA. Telephone (800) 221–5105.

Offers resources and referral information to persons who have lost a child to SIDS.

Parents of Murdered Children. 100 E. 8th Street, Room B041, Cincinnati, OH 45202, USA. Telephone (513) 721–LOVE.

Offers resources and referral support to parents whose children were murdered.

Rainbow Centre, 27 Lilymead Avenue, Bristol, BS4 2BY, UK. Telephone 0117 985 3343.

Counselling for children and families affected by life-threatening illness.

Rainbows for All God's Children. 1111 Tower Road, Schaumburg, IL 60173, USA. Telephone (841) 310–1880.

International; 4,000 affiliated groups. Establishes peer support groups in churches, schools or social agencies for children and adults who are grieving a death, divorce, or other painful transition in their family. Groups are led by trained adults. Newsletter, information, and referrals.

Samaritans, 17 Uxbridge Road, Slough, SL1 1SN, UK. Telephone 01753 532713. See telephone directory for local number.

Offers emotional support and befriending to the lonely, suicidal and despairing in complete confidence at any time of the day or night.

St Francis Center. 5135 MacArthur Boulevard NW, Washington, DC 20016, USA. Telephone (202) 363–8500.

This nonsectarian organization counsels and supports adults, children, and families; offers guidance to schools, religious institutions, and workplaces; and helps the community to respond better to those affected by loss. A significant service is the offering of training workshops on thanatology for professional and volunteer caregivers, clergy, and mental health workers.

Share. St Elizabeth's Hospital, 211 S. 3rd Street, Belleville, IL 62222, USA. Telephone (618) 234–2415.

National and international support group for parents who have lost a child, particularly (but not exclusively) through miscarriage, stillbirth, or newborn death.

Society of Military Widows, National Association of Uniformed Services. 5535 Hempstead Way, Springfield, VA 22151, USA. Telephone (703) 750–1342.

National nonpartisan group of widows and widowers of career members of the uniformed services whose purpose is to provide companionship, sympathetic understanding, and helpful advice.

Stillbirth and Neonatal Death Society (SANDS), 28 Portland Place, London W1N 4DE, UK.

Help to individuals or couples by way of befriending or group support from parents who have suffered a similar bereavement.

Tender Hearts. c/o Triplet Connection, PO Box 99571, Stockton, CA 95209, USA. Telephone (209) 474–0885.

International network of parents who have lost one or more children in multiple births. Newsletter information and referrals, phone support, penpals.

THEOS (They Help Each Other Spiritually). 717 Liberty Avenue, 1301 Clark Building, Pittsburgh, PA 15222, USA. Telephone (412) 471–7779.

International, over 100 chapters. Assists widowed persons of all ages and their families to rebuild their lives through mutual self-help. Network of local groups. Quarterly newsletter, chapter development guidelines.

Twinless Twin Support Group. c/o Dr Brandt, 11220 St Joe Road, Fort Wayne, IN 46835, USA. Telephone (219) 422–8642.

International network. Mutual support for twins who have lost their twin. Provides information and referrals, phone support, penpals, conferences. Newsletter. Group development guidelines. Provides assistance in starting local groups. Annual meeting.

Victim Support, Cranmer House, 39 Brixton Road, Stockwell, London SW9 5DZ, UK.

Practical help and advice and emotional support to victims following crime.

Bibliographies and publishing houses

Accelerated Development, Inc./Taylor & Francis Group, 1900 Frost Road, Suite 101, Bristol, PA 19007, USA.

Offers several books, video and audio tapes, and leader manuals for groups dealing with grief and loss.

Baywood Publishing Co., 26 Austin Avenue, Amityville, NY 11701, USA.

Offers a large selection of publications on death, dying, and loss.

Rainbow Connection; Compassion Book Services, 477 Hannah Branch Road, Burnsville, NC 28714, USA.

Acting as a consignment agency or broker for various publishers, this organization offers a large selection of books, videos, and audio materials on death, dying, grief, and loss.

Rudman, M.K., Gagne, K.D., & Bernstein, J.E. (Eds). (1994). *Books to help children cope with separation and loss: An annotated bibliography.* New Providence, NJ, USA: R.R. Bowker.

This volume includes over 740 recommended fiction and nonfiction 'real-life' situation books focusing on separation and loss experiences. For working with children aged 3–16.

Sounds True Catalog, 735 Walnut Street, Boulder, CO 80302, USA.

Offers video and audio tapes on dying, death, and mourning.

Magazines and professional journals

Bereavement: A Magazine of Hope and Healing. Bereavement Publishing, 1833 Telegraph Drive, Colorado Springs, CO 80920, USA.
Bereavement Care. CRUSE, Cruse House, 126 Sheen Road, Richmond, Surrey, UK.
Death Studies. Taylor & Francis, 1900 Frost Road, Suite 101, Bristol, PA 19007–1598, USA. Telephone (800) 821–8312. Also at Rankine Road, Basingstoke, Hants RG24 8PR, UK. Telephone 01256 813000.
Omega: Journal of Death and Dying. Baywood Publishing Co., 26 Austin Avenue, Amityville, NY 11701, USA.

Index